I'll Show Myself Out

Also by Jessi Klein

You'll Grow Out of It

I'll Show Myself Out

ESSAYS ON MIDLIFE & MOTHERHOOD

Jessi Klein

HARPER

An Imprint of HarperCollins*Publishers*

I'LL SHOW MYSELF OUT. Copyright © 2022 by Jessi Klein. All rights reserved. Printed in the United States of America. No part of this book may be used or reproduced in any manner whatsoever without written permission except in the case of brief quotations embodied in critical articles and reviews. For information, address HarperCollins Publishers, 195 Broadway, New York, NY 10007.

HarperCollins books may be purchased for educational, business, or sales promotional use. For information, please email the Special Markets Department at SPsales@harpercollins.com.

FIRST EDITION

Designed by Kyle O'Brien

Library of Congress Cataloging-in-Publication Data has been applied for.

ISBN 978-0-06-298159-2

22 23 24 25 26   LSC   10 9 8 7 6 5 4 3 2 1

For the mothers

Contents

The Hero's Journey...1

The Butterfly...13

On the Starbucks Bathroom Floor...31

Mom Clothes...45

The Car Seat...59

An Open Love Letter to Nate Berkus and Jeremiah Brent...69

Underwear Sandwich...81

My Future Lesbian Wife...89

Listening to Beyoncé in the Parking Lot of Party City...99

Somewhere over the Rainbow...111

Your Husband Will Remarry Five Minutes After You Die...119

Talismans...127

Bread and Cheese...137

Change of Hands...149

Hair...167

Contents

Teddy Ruxpin...185

Bad News...193

In Defense of Drinking...207

Eulogy for My Feet...217

Demon Halloween...225

Little Books...239

The Return...257

Acknowledgments...269

I'll Show Myself Out

The Hero's Journey

I'm driving the three-minute scoot to the supermarket to pick up a few boxes of very safe, instantly dissolving toddler cookies called Nom-Noms, which is really what all cookies should be called (and, while we're at it, all food). My two-and-a-half-year-old son, Asher, loves Nom-Noms, and we were about to run out, so this trip needs to happen before the shit hits the fan.

While in the car, I'm listening to the writer Elizabeth Gilbert on Oprah's *Super Soul* podcast (as you do). Gilbert is the author of *Eat Pray Love*, the 2006 bestseller about her soul-awakening travels to India, Italy, and Bali; it's a book I love and have read an embarrassing number of times.

Nom-Noms are these magical little biscuits that are probably about ninety-nine percent air. The rest is a mysterious blend of I think sweet potato juice and Styrofoam. (If you're thinking, *There's no such thing as sweet potato juice*, you are correct. But this is precisely the mysterious essence of the Nom-Nom.) Every Nom-Nom is reliably about five inches long and shaped like a mini surfboard with very minor irregularities around the edge. (I'm sure they could be baked to be perfectly smooth, but I think they're going for some kind of wabi-sabi "hand-hewn" aesthetic, which I appreciate in theory, but it also feels like an unnecessary effort given the audience?)

The day stretching out before me as I drove the three minutes from my house to the supermarket was itself a bit like a Nom-Nom; it would be the same as all the other days I've been living since my son was born, since we moved to Los Angeles, and since I've been working part-time. Part-time at home; part-time, occasionally, in an office; part-time, in an existential sense, as a mother; and the smallest part of the time, feeling like myself. My days look and taste a lot like nothing, and yet they are there. They mostly feel the same, but around the edges, of course, they are different.

The most colorful and sparkly, lovely differences are occasional boozy lunches with dear friends—truly, in my opinion, the greatest luxury of a self-employed person's life. But they are infrequent, partially because they feel too indulgent in the middle of the day, even though I know this is the rhythm of a writer's routine, and partially because everyone is busy. I'm supposed to be busy too, writing, and yet the paradox of being busy writing is that so much of writing feels dangerously similar to doing nothing. I sit and stare and, usually (again, this might be specific just to me), sink into a low-grade (but sometimes high-grade) depression. I have at it for as many hours as I can, the clock ticking down until it's time to go home. I'm supposed to relieve Asher's nanny at six p.m., but I always attempt to alleviate the guilt I feel about the number of hours our nanny works by letting her go twenty minutes early; I'm aware this is nonsense, and also I feel guilty for thinking this nonsense.

So anyway, Elizabeth Gilbert and Nom-Noms.

Gilbert was telling Oprah about how in the aftermath of *Eat Pray Love*'s publication, she was often approached, at book signings or talks, by two subsets of women. The first were those who, inspired by her book, bought plane tickets and attempted, in some fashion, to trace Gilbert's steps. (This group of women famously, if unintentionally, contributed to such a dense wave of tourism in Bali that it got to the point where there were almost more *Eat Pray Love* fans walking around than there were actual Balinese citizens.) The second subset—and this is the one that really caught my attention as I began my fifteenth circle around the supermarket parking lot, waiting for someone to leave so that I could grab a spot—was that group of women who had similarly been inspired to go on a spiritual globe-trotting quest by the book but were unable to do so for one of many reasons: the financial impossibility, a job that couldn't be left, a family or kids or sick parents under their care, or a combination of all of these things. Rapt, I parked my car and plugged in my headphones so I could finish the podcast while I was inside the store.

As I finally threw the Nom-Noms into my shopping cart, Gilbert was talking about the archetypal "hero's journey," and how throughout the history of literature, the hero's journey has been represented as, specifically, a man's journey to a faraway place. There, he conquers or fights some person or army or thing and, in doing so, saves us all. While this quintessential hero is running about, his wife/mother/sister/girlfriend/daughter/all of the above stays home, very much not on a hero's journey. She cooks or cleans or weeps or Pinterests while he is out and about, slaying and defending and generally being courageous. Though I was familiar with this trope (you're familiar with it too if you've ever seen, literally, any Hollywood movie—*Star Wars*, for example), I hadn't heard of the book Gilbert referenced at length, Joseph Campbell's *The Hero with a Thousand Faces*, in which he distills the seventeen universally traversed steps of this tale as it's been told forever by cultures around the world. I realize as a writer I probably should have read (or at least known about?) Campbell's book, but there are so many episodes of *The Bachelor* to watch that I'm not sure where I would have ever found the time.

As I waited on the checkout line, staring blankly at the displays of Altoids and magazines and realizing simultaneously that it was 4:23 p.m. and that nothing about my life felt familiar anymore, Gilbert started talking about how we need to reconceive our vision of the hero's journey. The hero's journey is not the exclusive territory of men, she said, and it does not have to involve faraway lands . . . I paused the podcast as I swiped my card to pay for the Nom-Noms.

Even after I loaded my recyclable bags (good person) into the back of my car and began the drive home, that concept and those words, "hero's journey," kept echoing inside me. Some lonely, estranged part of my old self, some thirsty little leaf, leaned toward the idea, wanting to know more. I find it harder and harder to read an entire book—dealing with a kid, *The Bachelor*, so very busy—but I can peruse the shit out of a long Wikipedia entry. So I googled "Joseph Campbell hero's journey" and started reading.

Campbell's conception of the journey begins with a potential hero, who is just going about his life as normal—you know, texting and taking antidepressants or whatever. He receives a "call to adventure," to a place that Campbell describes as: *"a forest, a kingdom underground, beneath the waves, or above the sky, a secret island, lofty mountaintop, or profound dream state; but it is always a place of strangely fluid and polymorphous beings, unimaginable torments, superhuman deeds, and impossible delight."* Reading this sentence gave me the same adrenaline-filled feeling you get when you are almost certain, but not yet positive, that you're feeling an earthquake—you freeze, and your whole body listens. In this moment of silent anticipation, for the first time since my son was born—having spent each day since feeling invisible to the mainstream world, over the hill, like a Swiffer on legs, wiping his nose with my hand, and not having sex, and generally functioning as a kind of automated milk-and-comfort-dispensing machine—I began to entertain a thought . . .

Is it possible I've been on a hero's journey this whole time? Is it possible I am on one right now?

What shook me about Campbell's words is how perfectly they describe motherhood. To begin with: a *"profound dream state."* The first three months after my son was born, for sure, were nothing less than a never-ending somnambulance. And even though I was not on a secret island or a lofty mountaintop, once I became a mom, I felt in my bones that deep sense of distance and isolation, of being far away from everyone else, stranded with my new *"strangely fluid and polymorphous being"*— i.e., my baby. If you've ever had a quality hang with a baby or very small child, you know a baby is as polymorphous as it fucking gets. Infants are from one minute to the next, by turns otters, mermen, humans, wombats, and puppies.

I don't think I even have to justify how *"unimaginable torment"* applies to child-rearing, but if you've ever had to physically wrestle your child into or out of a stroller, or if they've ever refused to go to sleep when you feel like you've literally passed away about two hours ago, you know what I'm talking about.

And of course, these are the exact same moments in which there is no more *"superhuman deed"* than steadfastly caring for and feeding your child and not giving in to the temptation to flee the entire situation. (There is a reason hospitals are now legally obligated to give new parents literature about "shaken baby" syndrome before they take a newborn home. It's not because they're so invested in ferreting out the one or two demonic people out of millions who might be capable of harming a child in this manner. It's because they know literally every single one of us, if we weren't informed that baby skulls are basically made of crème brûlée tops, and their brains are made of very small, even more delicate light bulbs that can shatter with the slightest bump, every single one of us, at some exhausted, delirious moment, would shake the baby.)

And then. Of course. The reason we don't shake our babies, the one thing that satiates us, even though more often than not it comes in infrequent, tantalizing little drips rather than a gushing faucet, is the *"impossible delight"* of being a mother. The impossible delight of having your seventeen-month-old child, out of nowhere, in the middle of an absolutely average day filled with building blocks, in which you are slowly evaporating inside from boredom, say to you for the first time, "I'm happy." And you cry, because this is why you chose his name: Asher, Hebrew for "happy," the emotion you've struggled so hard to feel your whole life.

So I have been thinking and thinking about this. Is it really possible that my trip to buy Nom-Noms is part of a meaningful narrative, a hero's journey? In trying to process it, I wonder why I've felt such inner resistance to accepting that anything I do as a mother might actually be a page in a book. And really, it doesn't take long to connect that feeling to the fact that in popular culture, at least in America for the past forever years, what mothers do is seen as so unremarkable it's not just an unimportant story, but not even a story at all.

To illustrate, I invite you to investigate your gut reaction to the term "mommy blog." Personally, I'll confess, it always strikes me as mosquito-ish, something small and trivial and undeserving of my attention. If this rings true for you as well, don't feel guilty; we've all just internalized that the word "mommy," when used as an adjective, automatically diminishes whatever noun comes after it. I guarantee you if Ernest Hemingway were alive and writing an online column about his experience of being a father, no one would call it a "daddy blog." We'd call it *For Whom the Bell Fucking Tolls.*

We think this about "mommy" because we live in a world where the majority of mothers we see on television usually pop up in detergent commercials and have triangle hair and don't seem to have any interests beyond keeping their kids' clothes absolutely pristine, which, by the way, is an unachievable and dare I say masochistic goal. Yes, I know it's just a commercial for detergent, so I understand these gals might not need a detailed, dramatic backstory highlighting their addiction to heroin in college. And yet you can actively sense that if this woman's life were, let's say, ever to be expanded upon in some kind of spin-off, it would still be about detergent and grass stains and nothing else. There is no story, there is no journey, there is only the stain of this moment followed by the stain of the next moment, going around and around like the washing machine itself.

In the weeks since I listened to Gilbert's interview, I've been realizing that the reason why starting to write this book has been such a heavy lift, and why it's led to so many afternoons of sitting and staring that look terrifyingly like doing nothing, is for this very reason: I've been paralyzed by the internalized fear of writing about being a mother. I've been worried that anyone picking up this book at the bookstore and flipping through its pages will see that there's Mom Stuff in it and immediately think that they are in detergent ad land, a land in which, of course, nothing ever happens that's worth reading about. Without fully acknowledging why to myself, I've desperately scrambled for something else I could write about—and please believe me, no one wishes more than I do that I could write about how I spent the last two years having an affair with a young cobbler I met on a nude beach in Ibiza. But that was not my last two years (or any of my years, if I'm being honest). My last two years were, nominally, Nom-Nom years. But since hearing Gilbert's talk, I know that while this is a part of the truth, it's also less than the truth.

The truth is that motherhood is a hero's journey. For most of us it's not a journey outward, to the most fantastic and farthest-flung places, but inward, downward, to the deepest parts of your strength, to the innermost buried core of everything you are made of but didn't know was there. And what I've learned, now that I'm finally saying fuck it and taking a Xanax to just calm down and suck it up and write this book: there's a reason motherhood as a story is so infrequently told.

It's because, for so many people, our safest, sweetest, earliest memories are of nestling in our mother's lap, in her rocking warmth, hearing her sing as we get milk-drunk and sleepy and burrow, heavy-eyed, into the crook of her soft arm. And if you knew that your mother's journey was, intrinsically, a hero's journey—if that was in any way an established narrative in our culture—you'd have to accept that this memory of womb-like safety, this foundation upon which so much of our identity is built, was often just an illusion. You'd have to realize that while you were blissed out on your mother's lap, one of those epic battles, the kind that envelops heroes as they fight their way out of a ring of fire, was raging just above your head. No one wants to believe that in the moments you felt the most peaceful, the woman cradling you so softly was shielding you from a sword that she herself was holding.

Every mother you know is in this fight with herself. The sword that hangs over you is a sword of exhaustion, of frustration, of patience run dry, of her bladder practically exploding like a water balloon as she enters her third hour of sitting in a chair trying to get you to sleep. It's the sword of missing a meal because there wasn't time to eat while she was packing a diaper bag with the endless amount of stuff you needed to go to the park; the sword of sneaking one bite of string cheese while sitting on the edge of a damp sandbox; the sword of indignation at how little she feels like a human when she so often has to look and behave like an animal. And mostly—and this is the spikiest truth—it is the sword of rage: the rage and shock of how completely she must annihilate herself to keep her child alive.

Ultimately, the hope of impossible delight almost always wins out over the impossible torment. I know this because here I am, alive, writing this, and here you are, alive, reading it, which means our mothers did what heroes do: they kept us all alive to tell our own tales one day. And what I can tell you is that so much of the heroism of motherhood is the ability to swallow the sword. To swallow the pain and frustration and keep everything inside. No one wants to think that their mother, that all-forgiving source of limitless unconditional love, occasionally, in a fit of rage or boredom, met her limits. And yet, of course she did. No one wants to know that after your mother finally placed you in your crib, she walked out of the room and screamed into a blanket, or cried in the bathroom, or drank a bottle of wine, or all of the above. No one wants to know that as she rocked you and sang you the tenth lullaby of the night, she was fantasizing about putting you down, walking out the door, and never coming back.

A mother's heroic journey is not about how she leaves, but about how she stays.

The Butterfly

I receive the email from Kidspace, the local children's museum that we occasionally visit and to which we have a membership because when you become a parent you will end up getting memberships to a million places you go about three times. It's butterfly season, and there will be butterfly kits for sale over the weekend. Grow your own caterpillar into a butterfly at home. This seems like a wonderful idea. A wholesome idea. Science and learning all wrapped up in a brief experience with a low-maintenance, beautiful pet. We have the book *The Very Hungry Caterpillar* and have read it hundreds of times, and this would be a chance to see it in action. One of nature's most miraculous transformations, plus a front-row seat to one of the world's favorite metaphors. Wings. For only fifteen dollars.

I have not been feeling like a good mother. Asher is now at an age where I should be teaching him . . . things. The part of his life where the only knowledge I had to impart involved letters and colors and numbers is over (we crushed it). Now the categories of what exists to be learned have expanded into infinity, an infinity that is even larger than when I was a child. I was born in 1975, and in 1975 all knowledge was contained in a set of twelve red encyclopedias that sat on the bottom bookshelf of my parents' bedroom. Stuffing all the knowledge in the world into these pages required a font the size of sand, but still, it fit. Maybe once or twice on a school project I tried to look something up in the index (its own volume) to find it not there, at which point I would decide that whatever I was looking up must not really matter or exist. But here we are in the twenty-first century, and there's forty-plus more years of history to know about. Thankfully we have the internet to teach us everything there is to know, but Asher is still too young for the internet, so until then, I am his internet. But it's hard to know what order to teach the internet in.

Butterflies seem like a good place to start. Even just thinking about this project fills me with a beatific sense of finally doing right. I don't often go out with my son just the two of us, because I'm scared of living in this city with almost no sidewalks; and even though I'm a good driver I don't feel safe driving with my son. We are almost never alone, actually. My plan is, I will take my son to the children's museum, we will have a wonderful afternoon, I will purchase our little caterpillar, and then we will nurture it together, looking at the butterfly, then looking at each other and quietly smiling, like we are in a commercial for some kind of church or organic diaper.

What really happens is none of this. What really happens is that Lucy, our nanny, takes Asher to the children's museum

14

and they buy the butterfly kit and bring it home. I imagine there will be some kind of lovely little artisanal habitat, like a Swedish crib, but what I find on my arrival home from work is a small clear tube, like a prescription pill bottle, the bottom of which seems to be lined with some kind of lumpy brown curd that truly looks like dog diarrhea. The caterpillar, instead of doing something cute, like munching on a leaf or journaling, sits upside down, frozen, under the cap. As I try to get a look at it, I remember that I am terrified of bugs. In the abstract I'd always thought a caterpillar's fuzziness makes it slightly more acceptable—closer to a very small, long dog—but on close inspection this caterpillar wasn't really fuzzy. His body had a rubbery appearance, and being able to look at him close-up I could suddenly make out his (her?) dotty little nightmare of a face, the two little whitehead eyes (oh God, are they eyes?) and some kind of black hole approximating a mouth. Touching a bug is out of the question for me, but even though there's a closed plastic wall between us, I am still deeply creeped out the moment the caterpillar moves and its feet are directly on the opposite side of the plastic from my finger. I put the tube gently down on the table, the hair on my neck fully standing on end. Still, I'm trying to be a great mom, an earth mother, so I ask Asher what he wants to name the butterfly.

"Buster," he says firmly.

I look at Buster.

"Welcome home, Buster!" I say.

Buster sits motionless on the ceiling again.

Good Lord, you're gross, I think.

Despite my full-body revulsion to Buster and his shit-filled tube-house, I still feel a protective motherly urge to make sure this caterpillar survives. That said, at this stage there is almost nothing for us to do. He is surviving on the dog-diarrhea food, and according to the instructions that came with the kit, all we need to do is wait for the moment where he goes to the top of the cap and hangs in a "J-shape," which will apparently mean he is letting us know it's time for him to turn into a chrysalis and we must airlift him (with cap) into an enclosure (they suggest putting mesh over an unlidded shoebox). When he emerges from the cocoon, he'll have to be in the shoebox for a day or two while his wings dry out (ew?) before he can be released.

Until that moment arrives, our main task seems to be keeping the tube out of direct sunlight, because Buster might fry. I fret about where to put the tube that will keep him cool. No matter where it's placed, it's a bit of an eyesore. He ends up on top of a cabinet in our dining room. The spot I settle on is safe from sun, but then I worry that Buster doesn't have much of a view. He is next to a stack of Jewish cookbooks. Oh well. Maybe it's fitting. His primary view is of the comings and goings of three Jews (two bigs and one little) and a woman from Mexico who cares for the little one. I am struck, over and over, at the mysterious universe that has brought us all together as roommates at this particular moment in time.

Every morning as Asher and I eat breakfast I tell him we

should check on Buster. We put his tube on the table and check on his progress. But he does not seem to be making any progress. Every now and then he has a little burst of activity, wiggling around, his tiny legs waving about here and there in a chaotic fashion, but for the most part, he is disturbingly still. I fret about what seems like the very tenuous line dividing a fun project about life turning into a morbid lesson about death. Asher still doesn't know what dying means, and I do not want to have spent fifteen dollars in exchange for being forced to have an existential discussion if Buster goes legs up.

So I check on Buster frequently, nervously peering into his tube late at night or early in the morning, the way I used to check on Asher when he was a newborn. Even though I should be relieved that he seems (for now?) to be alive, I am still frustrated that he doesn't seem to be advancing. He is here for one reason, to perform his one magic trick, and all the shit he's doing beforehand is kind of a bummer. It's like if you went to a Go-Gos concert and they refused to play "Vacation" and instead just did all their new stuff, and all their new stuff is just them frozen in a pill case covered in brown slime. *Fucking get on with it, Buster*, I think. I find myself nervously making jokes to excuse Buster's appearance when people come over. "Sorry about this," I say. "I realize it's not the most appetizing thing to look at." No one seems to care about him one way or another, but I am increasingly fixated. I'm annoyed he's not in his cocoon yet, but I'm also not entirely a monster—there's a part of me that feels a deep, empathetic claustrophobia on Buster's behalf. *He can't possibly be happy in there,* I think. I feel responsible for his plight. I'm part of the kids' museum industrial cruelty-to-animals complex that thinks it's okay for this little creature, gnarly as he may be, to be kept in a room only slightly larger than a thimble for so long. Normally, this process would be playing out in nature, in . . . well . . . I don't fucking know where caterpillars hang out while they're getting ready to get into cocoons. But maybe a field? A tree hole? It must be better than this. I don't really think about the conflict between my hand-wringing over his tiny cage and the fact that I am desperate for him to go into his cocoon, which is, arguably, the very smallest space a creature can be in, even smaller than the cage.

I am the only one in the family obsessed with Buster. But maybe that's because I am the only one projecting.

Buster is depressed, I think.

Asher is a few months away from turning four, and for the last few years, I have been in the rather tubelike experience of motherhood. I am twenty pounds overweight, and I feel out of place in Los Angeles, in my marriage, in my house, in my own skin. Even though I'm home all the time, I rarely feel at home. I am a person fully in charge of a small child who walks around doing mother-esque things, and yet I can never fully recognize this person as me. One of the staples of being the mom of a little kid has been that at least once a day, for me, there is some standard annoying little incident (nothing out of the ordinary, but when you have a child the ordinary has a way of feeling both insane and banal at the same time) that makes me fantasize about leaving the tube, the shoebox, my family, the whole thing. I mean, obvs, I would never actually leave—I'm just saying the FANTASY comes and goes.

Fortunately for me, I have a solo work trip back to New York City planned, and I am excited for four nights of hotel fully on my own. Before I had a kid I didn't know how amazing sitting at a hotel bar alone would be. Now it is one of the great joys of my life. I miss New York City in my bones; walking, looking, the feeling of bursting out a door onto a busy street filled with the completely unpredictable mix of humanity that is flowing down every block at every moment.

The morning I'm leaving, as I rush around at the last minute, throwing Ambien and USB cords into my suitcase, I tell Mike to take care of Buster, reminding him to keep him out of the sun, and about moving him to the shoebox when he becomes a chrysalis. Mike, of course, doesn't know anything about this. "Just read the printed instructions," I snip. He doesn't know where the instructions are. We scramble to find the crumpled instructions as my cab pulls up.

On my flight, I am worried about Buster.

I get to my hotel. I have stayed here a handful of times, so I don't know exactly where I stand as a "favored customer" or whatever, but I am dying to get a corner room because that's the kind of insufferable person I've become, and when the receptionist tells me the room I originally wanted isn't available, I say, "Ah oh well sorry to be a pain, it's just, you know, I'm a mom with a three-year-old at home and this is my little work trip away so gotta make the most of it," and I can feel as I say it that I hate myself but then they say there's an even nicer room for a higher price and I hear the price and even I have my limits and I'm like, "Sigh, no, never mind, Buster's gotta eat" (or does he?), and just then the receptionist is like, "Hold on," and the manager comes out and they clickity-clack a few more keys and suddenly they are saying, "You know what, we'll just give you the upgrade for the same price," and ohmigod I am on the twelfth floor with a corner bathroom and a corner bedroom and here I am, I made it, I am away from my family, I am alone, I am me.

Am I? I don't know who I am anymore, because this oddly now has become an away place and a not-me body, but I know that what used to be my body and what used to be me lived here, loved here, was here. I starfish out onto my bed, and from the bed I have a view of the Freedom Tower and the neighborhood where I grew up, and I hear waves of traffic and waves of people, and those are my ocean sounds, my womb sounds, what I heard when I was in my little New York City cocoon, lying awake at night, being created, for better or for worse, by all of this.

That night I eat a giant plate of pasta at the hotel bar for dinner and drink a martini and text with old friends. I sit on a couch in the lounge, half reading Mary Karr's *On Memoir* and half watching people who are inexplicably younger than me living lives there is now no chance of me ever knowing except in this one little moment that I am watching them saunter through the lounge to the cooler back of the lounge in that cool way that young people do where they sort of display themselves as they move through space and then make you feel bad for looking (somehow without even looking at you).

Afterward I take the elevator back up to my room, where I FaceTime with Asher. He is intrigued by the lights of the big buildings behind me. He is not used to these kinds of buildings, living as we do in squatter, darker LA. He is trying to figure out where I am and how I am his mom in such a different place, where it is night while he is still in day, while I am trying to figure out why I feel so different in the same place I lived for forty years.

"How is Buster?" I ask.

"Not in the cocoon yet," Mike says.

What the fuck, Buster? I think to myself.

It is the last week of April, which means I happen to be there for those precious few perfect days in a year that New York ever has. It's seventy-one degrees and ripe and bursting and the sky is bright blue and everyone is so desperate after a long shitty winter to be out of their down jackets that they've jumped the gun and are now just walking around basically naked. The whole city feels like it just woke up and is gonna start the day by gently thrusting around to see if anyone's into morning sex (everyone is). (Or it feels like everyone is.)

My first day I have two meetings five hours apart in Midtown and I'm exhausted, but there isn't really enough time to go back to my hotel and nap, so I decide instead to go to the Museum of Modern Art and walk around and be the person who is sitting alone having lunch at a museum in the middle of the day and just EMBRACE IT.

It's been close to a decade since I was last here, but as I walk through the museum I am hit by a wave of nostalgia. I have the sense memory of being a child and being here with my father when I was in grade school and then being here on my own in college, sitting on a bench looking at Jackson Pollock's *Lavender Mist*, one of his most famous abstract drip paintings, and feeling very deep I'm-looking-at-a-painting feelings. I pass the Joseph Cornell boxes, which I wrote my art history thesis on; I pass Joan Miró's *Birth of the World*. I am so happy to be here in this place where I spent so much time when I was younger, but it's almost as if the more beauty I see the more I feel the tide of nostalgia reversing backward into an ocean of something sadder than that, and I can't put my finger on it until I've had enough time to watch hundreds of other people doing what I'm doing, the tourists and the weirdo New York old ladies with their blue architect glasses frames and their geometric earrings and the people you expect to be here and the people you don't expect to be here. Everyone is moving so slowly, and no one is rushing, and it dawns on me, as the clock ticks away and it's almost time for me to go back onto the street and to my next meeting, that I am mourning the loss of the time in my life when I could endlessly indulge in the joyful selfishness of an afternoon doing nothing but looking at art. Just exploring the relationship between myself and someone's vision of beauty and not screaming at a young boy to stop throwing a toy Southwest Airlines jet at my face. I walk into the garden for my final few minutes and sit on a little wire chair and try to will the experience of the sun and the peace to remain in my body. I feel like the old me here, but I know it isn't quite real—it's like being in a dream in which you're being visited by someone who's died and it feels so vivid and you never want to wake up, but then, of course, you do.

The night before I come home, I'm FaceTiming with Asher when Mike appears on the screen to give me some news.

Buster's gone into his chrysalis, he says.

When I return home a few days later, I walk through the door, give Asher a huge hug, and then run to the kitchen to see Buster. I'm not quite sure what I'm expecting from a chrysalis. It's a beautiful word, one that evokes some kind of beautiful translucent orb, a Spielberg-worthy ET spaceship aglow with life. And yet, this is not what it looks like. What it looks like is a miniature rotten banana, slightly shorter than the length of my thumb, which hangs ever so tenuously from the ceiling of the shoebox to which he's been transferred. My dream of coming home to that ugly little worm in a plastic jar having being replaced with a bioluminescent art installation has been dashed as this whole experience has now somehow become an even bigger eyesore with a slightly larger footprint in our home.

Still . . . we are one step closer to the transformation I have been waiting for. The instructions say he should be in there for up to two weeks. During that time, I feel like an anxious husband with a very pregnant wife, powerless to do anything except hand-wring. I remain the person in the house most invested in Buster. Asher is three years old and checks on Buster with me once a day, but I don't think he has him on the brain, always, the way I do. I don't really know what Mike thinks about Buster because right now our marriage is strained and

I'm not entirely sure what he thinks about anything. That said, if I had to hazard a guess I would say he assumes everything will be fine and Buster will be fine because, not to generalize, but all men just assume things will stay alive with help from others. Maybe I am constantly thinking about Buster because in addition to the skittish experience of my eggshell marriage I've just finished a rather difficult job and haven't yet replaced it with a new one, so I have nothing but time to stare at Buster and fret. But you know the old saying, a psychotically stared-at caterpillar never hatches, so I try to distract myself.

In the morning I take walks around the reservoir near where we live. It's a nice enough walk, and in LA any kind of walk near your home is a blessing because walks are generally in short supply, but the frustrating thing is the path is a not-very-long two-mile circle that has some prettier parts, and some less pretty parts. There are eucalyptus trees and a view of the mountains and dirt path, which is nice for running (irrelevant for me since I have somehow become too old and tired to run). The consistently less-nice thing about it is that it's almost entirely enclosed by a high chain-link fence topped with razor wire, a holdover from when this reservoir actually held potable water that had to be protected. Now the water exists just for the view, which the fence kind of ruins. I recognize this is a rather pessimistic perspective, but I've recently become a view-half-blocked kind of person. I feel desperate for some unadulterated beauty in my life: in part, I'm sure, because LA has a kind of relentless strip mall ugliness to it; in part because I am still in the necessary drudgery of taking care of a very small child and my evenings are almost always in the house, moving through the two hours from dinner to bath to books and bedtime in excruciatingly small increments of time, marked by a trail of plastic toys that follows us from one room to the next.

I want to go somewhere and see something or do or feel something beautiful, but I feel trapped. Asher needs and wants me at night. I can't leave. I walk in my circles in the morning and try to focus on the mountains and not the fence. Every night I look at Buster and I can't help but think it's not going well in there. *Maybe this was a kid museum scam,* I think to myself, and then I think, *I'm a person who's looking at a chrysalis and seeing a scam perpetrated by educators.*

But then . . .

One morning I walk into the kitchen and look into Buster's shoebox home and I see him half in, half out. One bright orange wing has popped out, and the chrysalis itself has turned whitish and now seems to be simultaneously a part of and sliding off of Buster's new body, like a used condom mid-disposal. I yell for Mike and Asher and Lucy, and we all stare, because it is, honestly, amazing. Over the course of the day, the other wing pokes through, and then, when I'm not looking, at some point, Buster is just a butterfly, sitting very still on the floor of the shoebox. Lucy slides an orange slice into the box, per the instructions, as well as a little stick (I'm not sure of its purpose: Perch? Ambiance?). In any case, the final instruction tells us that after two or three days of his wings drying out, he will be ready for release back into . . . the wild? (Or whatever LA is. The City. Something.)

Mike and I agree that we need to prepare Asher emotionally for letting Buster go. While he may have been a temporary pet, he's still the only pet Asher's ever known. Over lunch, I tell him that soon Buster will be ready to fly away, and that it will be exciting and we should be proud that we helped him get to this point in his life. I tell him that we will need to encourage Buster. "What does that mean?" he asks. I think for a second. "It means we have to tell him we believe he can do it," I say.

The night before his release, I'm up long after everyone else has gone to bed. I look again at Buster, feeling so relieved we have gotten this far. Earlier in the day he was sitting on top of the orange slice, which made me happy in a way that was almost embarrassing. Right now he is on the floor of the shoebox again. He is still, but then gives his wings a little practice flutter. I know I don't know anything about butterflies, but he seems a little small to me. Do butterflies continue to grow once they're out of their chrysalis? He is orange and black, like a monarch, but still, he looks quite small. I wonder if he's really a moth. Maybe the museum scammed us by selling us a moth. Why even now am I worried that something about Buster isn't enough? Is he a beautiful enough butterfly? Do I have enough? Is trying to teach Asher about growth and life enough?

I should give Buster a fresh orange, I decide.

On Saturday afternoon, Mike, Asher, his babysitter Lara, and I ever so carefully, ever so gently, bring Buster's shoebox into the backyard. I quickly peel off the mesh from the front of the box, certain that Buster is going to make a break for it, and not wanting to feel his legs brush against my arm. But Buster just sits there. We are staring at him in silence. It can't feel great.

Then Asher says, "You can do it, Buster."

And the moment the words leave his mouth, Buster flies up like a shot out of a cannon. Asher ducks, a little scared and a little excited. Buster does one loopty-loop right before he goes over our fence, but then he goes over it, and over a tree, and he is gone.

It is odd how quickly I feel tears running down my face.

I didn't think Asher was paying attention when I told him what encouragement meant. But he was. He is paying attention to everything now. Everything I think he will miss, he catches, including the things I wish he would miss, like me glancing at my phone when we're playing cars, or me using one tone too snarky with Mike, or me in general struggling to stay present and be the mother my beautiful, sensitive son deserves. But every now and then he is actually listening to what I want him to, and for now he encouraged Buster to go. *You can do it, Buster.* The minute the butterfly heard that, he made his decision, and he was gone. Free. Of course he just needed a moment. Freedom is terrifying. But you can go after it anytime you want. It's so easy to forget. It's so easy not to be free.

We all need the encouragement of a friend.

For the next few weeks, Asher will occasionally ask me where I think Buster is right at that moment. "Where do *you* think he is?" I ask. He thinks he is maybe in a bush or a tree. Or on a leaf.

I don't know how long butterflies live, so I just tell Asher he's probably right, even though I assume Buster is most likely already dead. Whenever we see an orange butterfly, we both say, "Maybe that's Buster!" I wonder how long we will keep this up. Forever? But eventually, Asher stops bringing him up.

A few weeks later, after getting Asher off to school, I put on my shoes to go for a walk around the reservoir. I'm trying to remember exactly when it was, but I can't, because there aren't many emotional landmarks in my timeline anymore. I know that I went to New York, and we released Buster, but other than those things, I can only remember what I'm about to tell you. Everything else blends together without a lot of details: getting Asher into the bath, reading books, sweet handholds with Asher in bed, bickering with my husband, moving from Asher's room to my room, desperate for something to change, desperate for freedom, dreaming of a dramatic forward shift that brings me somehow back to that old me at the museum in New York City, just seeing beauty, being near it.

So what I'm about to tell you is this: I start walking on the reservoir path, looking at the mountain but walking next to that ugly fucking fence, and then all of a sudden, I see a little monarch butterfly, a bit on the small side, more like a moth, flying down from the sky. Fucking fuck, he genuinely looks just like Buster. He is fluttering above my head, like he wants to say hello, and it feels like such an impossible Disney movie cliché that it's almost making me laugh. And then he flutters lower and lower, spiraling downward, like a more elegant version of a doomed propeller plane, and lands on the ground directly in front of my toes. I stop moving, and crouch down and look at him. It's a perfect landing, insofar as he has landed on his many little legs. But now he isn't moving. He isn't moving at all.

He has died at my feet.

All that time waiting and waiting for Buster to stop being a caterpillar, to start being the other thing, to transform, wanting him to hurry, worrying about him dying before the big change.

Maybe, like Asher, he understood me even when I thought he wasn't paying attention. Maybe (but of course not, but does it matter if he meant it if I understand it anyway?) he just wanted to let me know.

Maybe he just came to remind me.

Maybe he just wanted to encourage me.

On the Starbucks Bathroom Floor

I am sitting on the floor of a handicapped stall in a Starbucks bathroom, and Asher is cowering against the door, his little jogger pants and new striped undies down around his ankles. I'm pleading with him, begging, there's nothing to be scared of, please, please, just sit on the toilet and pee. This drama began over twenty minutes ago, at which point I was still in a baseball catcher's crouch, before my knees began to hurt and I gave up and just full-on sat cross-legged with my butt on the tile floor and accepted I would be touching every possible surface of this public restroom.

Under the stall door, I see the feet of other women, women maybe in their twenties and thirties, coming in just to pee and/ or wash their hands (like normal adults). They will stop in for a moment and then go back to their lives. Maybe they will go have a drink or go fuck their boyfriends or go shopping or maybe they will just read a magazine on their couch and fall asleep. Whatever they are doing, I think about them overhearing this little drama unfolding next to them, and for just a fraction of a moment, I can remember what life was like before I had my kid, when I would pass parents and their small children having breakdowns. I would always see these people out of the corner of my eye, and I would take just enough emotional time to feel a combination of pity, irritation, and relief that I wasn't them. A child screaming on the floor was in the same visual category as seeing an overflowing public garbage can, a momentary eyesore—the product of careless people who I would not think about longer than it took me to pass by this blight. Now I'm aware that for these women, I am the overflowing garbage can. I am the public mess. But I'm also a person, and at this moment I'm feeling one million human feelings, many of which have to do with deeply wishing I could throw myself down one of those cartoon black circles that turns into a hole on the ground, one that will take me away from here, maybe all the way to China.

The second beat in the map of Joseph Campbell's hero's journey is known as the "refusal of the call." This occurs after the hero has, in one way or another, been tapped to take on an extraordinary challenge, one that involves crossing a threshold and leaving behind the life they have always known. Within the myth, the hero (who does not yet know they are a hero) decides he doesn't want to take on the challenge. Maybe it is too overwhelming, or too frightening. He decides he would rather continue on as he was, or is, and maybe someone else can take on this challenge, or maybe he hopes the challenge will just evaporate and resolve on its own.

This is how I felt when Mike started saying we needed to potty train our child.

Asher had just turned three and was still in a diaper. In fairness, so were several of his friends, but a lot of kids were now showing up for playdates at our house in undies. Mike had heard about a book that asserted there is a "window" during which a child displays interest in peeing in the toilet, a narrow moment of dispositional openness that occurs with the frequency of a full solar eclipse, and that this is the prime time for potty training; and if you "miss" this "window," and put off potty training after that interest has waned, you are forever fucked. Even as I told him this was ridiculous, I was haunted by Freud's writings on the psychological fallout of getting stuck at the anal stage of psychosexual development: becoming an anal-retentive obsessive, perhaps even a serial killer; or, on the opposite end of the spectrum, becoming an overbearing narcissist with a toxic aversion to boundaries, perhaps even a serial killer. Had I already doomed my child to one of these fates because I could not handle the challenge of teaching him to use the toilet?

I realize that if you do not have a child, you may have no idea what potty training entails. And even if you do have a child, if you are a man, it's possible you may have pawned off the bulk of figuring out this process to your wife (allow me to remind everyone here that I'm truly making no judgments because I AM THE ONE WHO TRIED TO PAWN IT OFF). If you are the wife, allow me to honor you and me both by detailing what we have been through.

Before you even begin the actual teaching process, you must go buy a book about potty training to use as your guide. Not only are you supposed to buy it, you're supposed to read it. Here is my review of all the books: They don't need to be books. They need to be pamphlets. All of these books are quite shockingly actual full-length BOOKS as if they were *On the Road* or *The Goldfinch* or *I Know Why the Caged Bird Sings*, things that you are reading for the pleasure and the expansion of your soul. I am not reading these books for pleasure or my soul; I am trying to get a child not to shit on a rug. Not to discourage anyone from writing these, to be clear—not only would I pay full book price for a pamphlet, I would actually pay exponentially more for brevity. A dollar per word not used. All I wanted was one bullet-pointed piece of paper describing the least amount of effort it would take to get Asher out of a diaper. Sadly, this did not seem to exist.

Mike and I both read one of the books multiple times and by chapter seven the author still had not gotten to how to potty train. Chapter three of the particular book we had purchased was just the warning not to miss the fucking window. MAYBE YOU MISSED THE WINDOW FOR MY

INTEREST IN YA DUMB BOOK. In any case, even with a highlighter, I had to keep going back to understand the phases and the timing, and the only thing worse than having to read a whole book on potty training is having to reread it multiple times.

Between the book and the internet, we finally assembled an idea of what we had to do. What to do first (after buying and hating a book) is buy a short little plastic toilet that will be your child's practice potty. It has a removable bottom, removable because after your child pees or poops in it, you wash out the pee and the poop. With your hands. I know we had been doing diapers forever, and diapers are filled with poop and pee, but that seemed to me like a cleaner situation than having to wash something in the sink, as if it were a plate, when in fact it had been used as a toilet. The whole thing is revolting.

The training would begin in earnest with a "boot camp" weekend during which—horror of horrors—we were not to leave the house. Asher was supposed to wear a shirt, but no diaper and no pants.* Being able to see his pee and poop (should they be excreted away in an environs other than the toilet) would make him aware that their new place of belonging was, in fact, the sewer vis-à-vis the bathroom. The idea of entertaining my half-nude child indoors for forty-eight straight hours

---

* A look I've always known as "Porky Piggin' it," although the toilet training books do not call it that.

sounded about forty-eight times worse than the idea of having to entertain my clothed child indoors for one hour, but the point was to stay close to the bathroom so he could be airlifted to the bowl the second he had to go. I tried to bargain with Mike—couldn't we do just a quick outing or two?—but he is an exacting rule follower and felt that to leave the house for even a moment—a second—would ruin everything. This is not shocking as, again, he was the same person who believed in the calamitous consequences of potentially missing "the window." But as a "window" skeptic, I continued to push back. We fought about whether we could step out of the house for even a moment like two rabbis arguing the finest points of kosher law—which is to say, we ran microscopically pointless differences into the ground.

The level of claustrophobic panic just contemplating this process gave me cannot be overstated. It felt like planning a multi-leg flight to Australia without ending up in Australia at the end. It felt like being dropped into a lobster cage. It is not easy to write those words. I realize they make me sound like a bad mother. I am aware that this whole book makes me sound like a bad mother. And yet I'd be lying if I told you that the anticipation of this journey didn't fill me with dread. I felt a kind of rage at the phrase "potty training," with its minuscule and cutesy affect, like something unrelated to real effort or even real people. The fact that I hadn't read anything by other women (or men or anyone) relating a similar depth of feeling around this milestone made me feel even worse for wanting to escape so badly. Maybe a definition of "bad mother" is someone who thinks too much about the time when they weren't one.*

When the potty arrived, I took it out of the box and then out of its plastic sleeve. There had been multiple colors of plastic available, and somehow I had chosen teal, which in the moment had seemed like the best option, even though teal is generally the worst option unless you are designing a uniform for a Florida-based sports franchise, in which case, people always seem to love the worst option?

For a moment, this hideous teal toilet and I regarded each other skeptically. This was the call to my hero's journey. It was not as iconically cinematic as a hologram visitation from Princess Leia, but nevertheless, the arrival of this plastic eyesore, assembled in some distant Chinese province and sent under Amazon's direction to my doorstep, was my call.

---

* I mean, as long as we're here, sure, I'll tell you about the time my writer-director friend called me and asked me to do a very, very small role in the movie he was making. I have no confidence as an actor, so I asked him to tell me about it to make sure I could handle it, and turns out the "role" was to play a woman at a party giving Mark Ruffalo a blow job. I know. I KNOW. I quickly responded that yes, I could find it in myself to figure out the motivation for this role. What occurred next was, I spent a day with Mark Ruffalo, who, quite simply, was one of the most beautiful, kind men I have ever met. We had to be in a concrete stairwell with me on my knees pantomiming giving him a blow job, and truly he was more caring and concerned about me than men to whom I have given actual blow jobs. At one point he turned to a PA and asked if they could bring me a pillow to put under my knees. A PILLOW TO PUT UNDER MY KNEES. He didn't even know me!

And I refused it. Or at least, I postponed it. I stuck it under my son's bathroom sink and walked away.

One night, a few weeks after I hid the potty, Asher was goofing around after his bath. He pulled the potty out from under the sink. He looked at it for a moment, and then peed directly into it. Swish. Nothing but net.

Mike and I looked at each other. The window, Mike said, was open. It was time.

The Friday night before our no-pants no-exit weekend, I went to the pharmacy to see if there were any refills left on my Xanax prescription. There were not. Hm, ha, what a mystery, how did that happen? It was already too late to call my doctor without having to declare this situation as an emergency to her answering service. I mean, it absolutely WAS an emergency, but I was feeling a bit sheepish about how fast I'd gone through my prescription, so I was on my own. I started going through every purse and suitcase in the house, looking to see if there was even a crumb of Xanax to be found, perhaps some Xanax dust stuck in a dopp kit zipper, and eventually sculpted a little Xanax golem out of broken-off pieces in an old bottle I found at the back of Mike's medicine cabinet (yes, we're a two-Xanax-prescription family).

Saturday morning arrived. The moment I heard Asher wake up, I swallowed my drugs and we began the program. We had purchased new puzzles, new board games, kid versions of indoor bowling pins. Asher happily darted about with no pants. I had also purchased him a slightly longer T-shirt, one that hit mid-hip, for a little modesty. It looked kinda like Alvin and the Chipmunks were having a coke party in a Vegas hotel room.

The physical tells of him having to relieve himself were extremely clear, and after the first few gentle shoves toward the plastic potty, a Hanukkah-level miracle occurred: he seemed to get what he was supposed to do almost immediately. As predicted by the book (maybe I was too hard on the book?), sacrificing this one weekend seemed to have actually . . . worked? By Sunday morning, I was helping him into a brand-new pair of little striped undies. Holy fuck. I felt guilty that I had been such a downer about this and that I had postponed it for so long. We were all fucking geniuses. We had done it!

Except we hadn't.

On our first family outing to the park, with Asher in his newly slim, diaper-less silhouette, we played for an hour before the telltale signs of him needing to pee appeared. The fidgeting and crotch touching and dancing around. Mike tried to take him to the bathroom. They were gone a few minutes. Then they came back out. "He won't go," he said, brow furrowing.

"Asher, do you have to go to the bathroom?" I asked.

"No! I want to go home!" he shouted with his hand down his pants, then started hitting us, as one does when one is hiding that they have to pee. We packed up his sand toys and hustled to the car. We drove home and ran into the house, where he urgently beelined to the bathroom and obediently peed a titanic amount into the teal potty. "Okay," I said as at least half a gallon of urine streamed. "Next time you go in the potty at the park, okay?"

And this is where we got stuck. Asher absolutely refused to use a public toilet. At first I thought it might just have been the bathroom at the park, because who could blame him, it's disgusting. But it wasn't. It was all of the toilets in the world that weren't the plastic teal potty at home. He wouldn't go at school, he wouldn't go at a restaurant, he wouldn't even go at a friend's house. He just... held it. Every outing became a ticking time bomb, taking him to a place until he would feel the need to urinate, at which point he would always refuse to go to the bathroom, insist he didn't need to go, but then also start crying that he had to go home. There is nothing as simultaneously stressful and infuriating as watching a little person who won't stop gripping their crotch with both hands insist that they don't need to pee. (I'm not sure if "gaslighting" is a term that applies here, but I'm using it anyway. It's fucking gaslighting.) I would try to convince him, pleading, cajoling, reasoning, and begging, all of which inevitably ended with me giving in and strapping him into the car and then racing home so he wouldn't piss in the car seat.

I wondered if we should be bringing the plastic potty with us on outings, as I'd seen other families taking one out of their cars' trunks at toddler soccer and letting their kid piss or crap in it a few feet away (but never enough feet away) from the field. I couldn't bring myself to do this. It was one thing to no longer be the me who once got to spend a day pretending to blow Mark Ruffalo, it was another thing to drive around with a fucking toilet in my car. I just could not. I asked Mike if he thought we should put Asher back in diapers when he went outside, and he got furious. He really didn't act like Mark Ruffalo at all.

I spoke to one of Asher's preschool teachers about how he refused to go to the bathroom when we were away from the house, and would only use the plastic potty at home. "Oh," she said. "You shouldn't have gotten that. Those things only make the whole process harder."

What the fuck are you talking about? I thought.

"What?" I said.

"Well, because then you have to really potty train them twice, once with the plastic thing and then again with real toilets."

.

.

. . .

!!!!!!!!!!

Dark night of the soul.

After over a month of this, we couldn't take it anymore. We devised a plan to ply him with juice to the point of bursting, and then take him to Starbucks, where we would force him to pee in their restroom. This is not a plan that is discussed in any of the books, most likely because it is, if not technically child abuse, kinda similar? Mike said that I should be the one to take him to the toilet because at that moment he would "need his mother" emotionally.

Which brings us back to where we began, under the fluorescent lights in the one handicapped stall of the Starbucks bathroom. When we first walked in, I was resolved to be patient. Calm and clear. A rock. But the minute I told him he would have to use the toilet, he started clawing at the door and whimpering. I wouldn't let him out, and the whimpering soon turned to full-on hysterics. One by one, all of my planned tactics fell away as he resisted my standard pleading, cajoling, reasoning, and begging. It was as if we were in a terrible one-act play, with him perfectly cast as a three-year-old refusing to use the toilet and me horribly miscast as a mother. Various audience members (aka the other women using the bathroom) walked out of this show as quickly as possible.

The moment that I raised my voice, and told him in no uncertain terms that we were not leaving this stall until he had at the very least sat on the toilet, he began to wail a heartbreaking, tremulous sob, his mouth flipped fully upside down as he gasped out these terrible words:

"Mama, I'm scared! I'm scared! I'm scared, Mama!"

What I had forgotten, while wandering in my own night, was that Asher was on his own hero's journey. And although our journeys were intertwined, paradoxically, this particular moment was about us separating. Deep down, in his three-year-old heroic soul, Asher's terror wasn't truly of the toilet. What was happening involved the bathroom, but underneath, it was really about crossing another threshold of being on his own. The day the umbilical cord was cut, a tiny space was created between us. Now it was about to grow in as profound a way as any that had occurred since then. He, not I, would be in charge of the most vulnerable parts of his anatomy; and he would be, in the most primal way, in charge of trusting himself. Sadly, in this department, as with many others, I am a terrible role model. My lack of faith in myself was part of the reason I had been running from this whole process. I wasn't sure I could steer this ship. I wasn't sure I knew how to do any of this. It felt as impossible for things to change as it felt for them to stay the same. I didn't know if I could withstand the mess we would make as we lurched forward. And in this particular moment, crouched next to the Starbucks toilet, I was absolutely no match for my son's wrenching heartbreak over where we were, and where we had to go, which was ultimately further and further apart. Giving birth to him had launched him into my orbit, but with the revolution of every passing day, my little satellite would always be inching further away from me, until the day when I would cross the very last threshold of my journey, and I would have to fully let him, and everything else I know and love, go.

I have been thinking about why the refusal of the call is as important a beat in the hero's journey as the moment she embarks. It feels counterintuitive—after all, don't we always just want a story to get going as quickly as possible? Why do we need to see someone not doing something before they do it? Perhaps because acknowledging the depth of fear that reaching the edge of the known creates within us is as much the value of any story as the final triumphs. Maybe honoring the terrifying moment before crossing a threshold, the passage of life in which we are at a between and must summon our bravest, deepest selves to move forward, is as nourishing and curative to an audience as the moment of a victorious return home. Because somehow, nothing ever feels lonelier than changing, even though it is the thing we are all constantly doing. All around the world, from all walks of life, people are saying one version or another of "Mama, I'm scared." If we don't pause and acknowledge the fear, we miss the very stakes our hearts are rising to meet.

We left Starbucks without him peeing in the toilet, both of us red-eyed and agitated. I bought us each a biscotti, though, which helped.

As I write this, he is four and a half. I don't remember exactly how long after the Starbucks one-act play he finally got over his fear, but it wasn't much later. It just happened. I remember the details of the not doing it so much more than the doing. He goes to preschool now from eight thirty a.m. to two thirty p.m., and I am still getting used to the fact that he has an entire half day away from us, a day with other people, about which, even if he shares a lot of details, we can only ever get a tiny sense of what happened, a puddle's worth of reflected sky. My heart still skips a beat when he uses the words "my friends." Today, after dropping him off, I worked from home. The house was empty. Around one o'clock, eating some eggs off a plate, I looked out the window and just missed him terribly.

Mom Clothes

For at least the first year after my son was born, I wore the same thing every day: an ankle-length stretch cotton skirt with an elastic waist from Splendid (I had two, one in navy and one in gray), and one of two borderline-acceptable shirts, either an asymmetrical long T-shirt from Free People or a J.Crew button-down that had nothing to recommend it except the fact that I could easily pop my boobs out to feed my child. Anchoring this smokin'-hot lewk was a pair of dirty blue Toms slip-ons that I bought while I was pregnant because I'd ceased being able to bend over to tie my shoes. Other than occasionally rotating in the one pair of maternity jeans that vaguely made me look like a human, that was truly it for a year. My look fell somewhere between Orthodox Jew and hobo.

The underlying problem was that I'd gained fifty pounds while I was pregnant and had naïvely assumed I was somehow carrying fifty pounds' worth of baby that would all be gone the minute I pushed my kid out. Of course, I knew the baby did not weigh fifty pounds, but I thought he'd be about eight pounds and then the other forty-two would just messily pour out in the form of something like Styrofoam packing popcorn, as if giving birth were akin to opening a box containing a fragile lamp. Well, oopsie, was I wrong, because the weight I was carrying turned out to be mostly due to food I'd eaten. And it did not "come out" when I gave birth, mainly because it seems to have very much been incorporated into my stomach and butt. For the first few weeks after Asher was born, I hoped in vain that it would all somehow evaporate, but—spoiler alert—it did not.

For a month or so, I made do with my maternity dresses and a few large T-shirts that I could just sausage myself into. I'd heard that sooner rather than later, all the baby weight would just "melt off" with breastfeeding. The other thing I'd heard was that if all the weight didn't vanish with the breastfeeding, then at the very least it would slip away the minute I began "chasing the baby around." This is Fake News, and Shame on Me for not knowing better and not having observed, by that point in my life, that babies do not move from one spot for at least six months.

As I was not magically losing weight, I was left sartorially stranded on a lumpy island somewhere between my maternity clothes, which were tents, and my prepregnancy clothes, which no longer fit at all. The Splendid skirts and button-downs became my forgiving, if unflattering, lifeboat. The only thought that comforted me was that of course this is what most other new moms I encounter will be wearing because we are all currently in the same place, right? I looked forward to going to the park with my child and feeling a sense of sisterhood with my fellow matronly castaways.

This sense of shared destiny, however, was not to be. I was naïve, I suppose, not to realize that Los Angeles, with its collective female body mass index of negative-eight, would be a different world. Nonetheless, I still vividly remember my shock when I first schlepped Asher's stroller out to the park on a hot summer day. I didn't wear my Splendid skirt because I knew I'd be spread-eagled out on the ground with a crawling baby, and so I had to resort to the non-heat-friendly maternity jeans and a giant T-shirt of Mike's that he never wore anymore because it wasn't nice enough for him.* I made it to the rim of the sandbox, plopped my kid into the sand, and looked around for a similarly shlubby comrade (mom-rade?). The first woman I saw was wearing fucking espadrilles with body-conscious overalls, the latter of which I hadn't even known was a thing? She was there with her friend, another Instagram-ready #nofilter natural beauty in perfect white shorts and some kind of artisanal, locally sourced, environmentally sustainable blouse. Both of them had small boobs that seemed somehow unaffected by gravity or nursing. How was this possible? To be clear, these women appeared to be my age; I wasn't doing a cruel mental who-wore-it-better exercise comparing myself and a teen.

---

* Mike is a good dresser and has great taste; I'm obvs not blaming him for this, but it was a bit insult to injury that while my postpregnancy body had landed in baseball field–sized tarps, he was still swanning about in his REGULAR PANTS. From VINCE!

They were probably about forty, which is why it was so personally horrifying that they both looked, if not exactly like Gwyneth, then Gwyneth-adjacent. Have I mentioned their boobs? I couldn't understand it. I felt an irrational sense of annoyance, which, as I examined it, bubbled into something even worse, something closer to anger.

It's a terrible feeling to be mad at another woman for being thinner than you. It's terrible because it stems from an involuntary, internalized patriarchal self-loathing that just gets projected outward. Then you loop around the self-loathing track once again because you can't control this stupid reflexive jealousy. What fun! Of course, as a woman, I've been around this barn before—the seeing and yearning followed by the toxic resentment of both my fellow women and myself. But somehow being postpartum made it all worse. I'd thought that maybe just for this one phase of life we'd all be hanging out together with our leaking, giant boobs and our freshly flappy stomachs, that pregnancy and new motherhood would be the great fashion equalizers and force us all into loose tube skirts and blousy peasant tops that started wide at the top and just got wider and wider as they went down.

But some women's bodies just snap right back after pregnancy, without any effort. It's not their fault or my fault or anyone's fault. I can tell you think it's someone's fault. IT'S NOT! Is someone screaming? Oh, I guess it's me. The point is, these women at the park seemed relaxed, rested, and adorable. Sexy, even. I will say that one of the more useful developments in my personality since having my son has been a generalized giving of way fewer fucks, but especially about what I look like; a stubborn, feral sense of being too focused on keeping a little totally dependent person alive allows me to mostly disengage from concerns about my own appearance. But I'd be lying if I said this wasn't part of the constant battle within myself, this interior wrestling match between the new, wild id of motherhood and the old teenager-ish self that never stops feeling desperately inadequate.

This high school version of me inwardly pouted about how absolutely unfair it was that these women were around a children's park daring to have made an effort. But I've lived enough years to know that thinking life is unfair is the closest your own brain can come to making a noise that sounds like whining, and it's usually a clear signal that the time has come to shut your mouth and start actually doing something. In this case, the clearest thing to do about the unfairness of not effortlessly losing the fifty pounds you gained while pregnant, if you wanted to lose it, would probably be to go to a gym.

Here's the thing, though, about trying to exercise while you have a baby: it's mostly impossible. I didn't get this before I had a child. I vaguely remember thinking that I understood that moms must not have time to work out, but I realize now this is like saying you fully understand the theory of relativity because you once were on a train and looked out the window. Lack of time is only half the story. Because even if, should you have the privilege of being able to afford a nanny or day care or some other caregiver, and you are able to make the time to exercise, the thing I didn't anticipate was the *sheer unending exhaustion of having a baby.* All of this is to say, I used to have trouble motivating myself to work out when I didn't have a child. If I was hungover or even just a skosh sleepy, or if there was a slight breeze, I'd immediately take off my bra and lie down. Little did I know that what felt like insurmountable inertia then was *fucking nothing* compared to what was to come.

For the first six months of his life, Asher woke up at least three times a night, if not four. The days that followed were fully lost, zombie stupors where even though my body was physically at work, my mind was sludge. Even when he started sleeping through the night, he was such an early riser that I had to go to bed by 9:30 p.m. so that I could function when, like clockwork, he would start making noise at 4:46 a.m. Also, I'm being generous when I say he slept through the night because that really occurred maybe fifty-one percent of the time. There were still middle-of-the-night interruptions: bad dreams and fevers and colds and just the endless baby stirrings that babies cook up.

For those first two years, the sleep deprivation would often knock me out flat. One of the most disconcerting experiences of motherhood is to have so many precious days of your limited life span be reduced to a kind of waking static in which you're so bone-tired that the day becomes essentially just one long, soggy pause between getting the baby up and then getting both of you down. In this wet-cotton-ball state, the notion of exercising wasn't just something I didn't want to do, it was . . . just, no. A pass. I mean, I could *not.* I know that there are many women who somehow make this happen, and I regard them with the same sense of pure awe and wonder as I do the people who built the Great Wall or those Easter Island heads.

Around my son's second birthday, I realized that I was not going to be fitting back into my pre-baby clothes anytime soon, and, if I was being real with myself... ever. Ironically, this only dawned on me when I finally was able to lose a few pounds. Like an idiot, I eagerly pulled out some of my old clothes thinking I'd just slip right into them like in Days of Yore. What I discovered as I tried to wrestle an old J.Crew top over my chest was that my body had not only gotten bigger, it had fundamentally changed shape. Even if I lost all the weight I'd gained, breastfeeding had shifted a significant percentage of my body mass into my boobs in such a way that the type of top I used to wear was now, to put it politely, off the table. Upon closer inspection, the majority of the items in my closet had been hanging untouched for about two years as I waited to somehow turn back into the person who wore them and hadn't been pregnant. But how long are you supposed to wait? At what point do you accept that this ex-boyfriend (your favorite dress) is never going to fuck you (fit you) again?

One night, in a fit of manic frustration, I decided to part with every single thing that no longer fit. I realized how much of my wardrobe I'd bought in 1998—and I'm not talking about vintage leather jackets or anything that makes sense to hang on to. I mean that I still have "pieces"* I bought at Old Navy when

---

* When people refer to fancy clothes as "pieces" I always feel like throwing a chair.

I was trying to be presentable as a freshly college-graduated temp.

This closet purge turned into a deeply nostalgic walk (of shame) down memory lane. Every dress, every skirt told a story. There was the short green cotton dress with a low V-neck that had spanned a million unsuccessful dates, and that was then redeemed when I wore it (with fishnets and a pair of gray wedges, which made no sense) to my then-boyfriend-now-husband's fortieth birthday dinner. It had been part of a little splurge at Betsey Johnson a million years ago, which included a tiered short chiffon dress with beaded spaghetti straps. I remember feeling like I was VERY hot shit in this dress, and maybe I was a little bit, because it's what I was wearing when I finally made out with a British colleague I'd had a huge crush on at a work party.*

I emptied my drawers of jeans and cute little Anthropologie sweaters that now looked absurdly small, like they'd belonged to a doll. These had all felt so expensive and important when I bought them, and had in their own way become a part of my identity. But becoming a mother alters every inch of your body, your routine, your soul, your heart. This makes sense,

---

* We went back to his rental town house in the West Village and he lifted me up onto his kitchen counter and made a friendly attempt at taking my clothes off, at which point I remembered that my pubic hair was completely untamed and poking out both sides of my Hanes Her Way underwear. Embarrassed, I had to reverse course and feign modesty, like I was someone who didn't want to have kitchen counter sex right away with her European coworker.

of course: How could the arrival of a baby not change these things? Yet somehow I wasn't prepared for the idea that I would have to shed, essentially, almost every item of clothing that had defined me for the past two decades.

So now, at an exceptionally ragged forty-one, I was faced with having to buy all new clothes, which, aside from being a big expense, was also an exercise in figuring out what I was supposed to look like now. (I suppose I should be saying "*who* I was supposed to look like" but if you had seen me, truly, I was closer to a "what.") Were there new rules I was supposed to follow? Because I'm lazy, and also because like most people I was a bit attached to the person I had been most of my life, I decided I wanted to look pretty much exactly the way I had before, just three sizes larger.

This was my plan until I went to the mall and woke up to the rude reality that most of the stores I'd gone to in the past no longer carried clothes that fit me. With my waist at a size 12/14, I was suddenly at the very last stop on many major chains' sizing lines before being asked to get off the train and reboard the shuttle to the lady version of big and tall stores, which is, of course, the hottest pile of steaming bullshit because the average American woman is a size 16. I know this is not news, but it seems to bear repeating at top volume from every possible rooftop because none of these stores appear to be listening. Many department store labels don't even stock sizes beyond an 8, so essentially, if you're more than a burrito heavier than the largest person you've ever seen in *Vogue*, you're shit out of luck.

Replacing my old stuff would not be possible. I'd have to

reimagine who I was, what I'd look like when I walked out the door, what I wanted to project. And time was running out because both of my Splendid skirts, my MVPs, were starting to come apart at the seams, as if in addition to being skirts they were also mood rings.

It would be hard enough to figure out a brand-new style on a body that was familiar, but now I had a mom bod, complete with giant boobs and a bigger butt and a general thickness that wasn't there before. Even more than the physical changes, though, was the question of how my new status as a mom would (or wouldn't be?) present in my appearance. Was "dressing like a mom" inevitable? Was I doomed to look like one of those Tide ad matriarchs in their laundry-doing outfits? (I want to be clear, I'm not putting down women who choose to dress this way; however, I am quite down on the ad men within the detergent industrial complex who've decided that the only people who do laundry are women, and the only women who do laundry are mothers, and the mothers all wear matching twinsets as if they were in some kind of cult, and that cult worships doing laundry?)

This is where the city of Los Angeles, which in some ways had emotionally accelerated this whole crisis, actually redeemed herself. I'd lately noticed, as I strollered Asher around the neighborhood, a particular women's fashion that I'd never really seen while I was living on the East Coast. It involves a kind of oversized, loose-fitting linen silhouette. Sometimes it's separates, like a wide-legged Gumbyish pant and a sheath-like tank top; or sometimes it's a full-on '70s caftan, the type of thing

Jim Morrison would have worn to read a book on the sunporch. It's Stevie Nicks witch vibes but with more breathable, warm-weather-friendly textiles. There's a dash of sister wife in there as well, just to finish painting the picture. In the last few years, one-piece jumpsuits or rompers have become one of the most popular staples of this style as well. I was initially skeptical of this look; they all seemed to be a poop chute away from being toddler pajamas—not that there's anything wrong with toddler pajamas, and in fact the lack of crotch flap on the adult jumpsuits actually seemed like an oversight?

But then one day I wandered over to this annual event in my hood called the Echo Park Craft Fair. I was picturing the kind of New York street fair where tube socks are sold in a bag of ten pairs for four dollars, which as far as I'm concerned is the only appropriate packaging and price point for socks. However, this fair turned out to be a collection of the most rarefied, preciously twee, peak LA pseudo-shamanic objects you've ever seen in your life: Hand-hewn clay vases. One-inch-wide brass bowls in which to store seeds—or weed? Or weed seeds? Japanese block-print pillow covers. The only thing that cost four dollars was the ticket to get in. It's all so LA, which is to say, it's ridiculous. That said, I secretly wanted to buy all of it. The fair was packed, and all around me women were dressed in the sister-wife style I've described. Young and old, thin and less thin, moms and non-moms alike were all walking around in this cultlike garb. Everyone actually looked attractive, but moreover—deeply comfortable?

In one particularly teeming corner of the fair, there was a

popular vendor selling a lot of these kinds of threads, and I finally decided—just for a second, no strings attached, low presh, no presh—to throw on a linen jumpsuit, just to see how it felt.

I looked in the mirror.

The jumpsuit had four pockets, two on the chest, two on the hips—pockets for a cell phone or string cheese or car keys or a monkey lovey or mace, all my womanly/motherly needs.

It was loose, but not in a tent way. It was—what's the euphemism?—forgiving.

My flappy mom stomach and butt were tastefully draped and hidden from view.

Did I mention the pockets?

And, of course, I was as comfortable as I'd been since, well, since I was a toddler, free from the constraints of hard seams or button-dependent pants.

I bought the jumpsuit. I figured I'd give it a try.

After wearing it around for a few days, I realized that not only was I in love with the jumpsuit, but it was all I ever wanted to wear every day for the rest of my life. I loved that it wasn't trying to be sexy or chic. It wasn't even trying to be considered clothes for daytime, or public exposure, or even really clothes. By being so aggressively out of the game, it was, in a way, a uniform of gentle retirement, a quiet exit from effort. And yet, ironically, it was so completely unsexy that it circled back to suggesting, if not quite allure, then the confidence of someone possessing allure. It's a fine line between a woman wearing an adult onesie because she's embarrassed about her body and a woman wearing an adult onesie because she's so confident about her body she doesn't need to *not* wear an adult onesie. The sexual intrigue is in the guessing, if that makes sense? I mean, which one IS she? Only the luckiest gentlemen will find out!

Years later, I'm still wearing the jumpsuits. I now have them in five colors: dark denim, light denim, sage, royal blue, and black. This is going to sound slightly insane, but I've worn them so frequently the last few years—dare I say, almost every day—that they have felt almost like friends, supporting me at difficult times.

As I write these words, we are emerging from a global pandemic, during which everyone who was privileged enough to work from home basically dressed, if not in loose jumpsuits, then definitely something spiritually similar, for a year. Now people are excited to be putting on "real clothes" again, and for the first time in a very long while, I find myself wondering if I'm really sticking with the jumpsuits as my forever look. Is it time for a change? Have I outgrown this uniform? The other night I went to a dinner out with friends, one of my first after fifteen months of quarantine, and as I was getting ready, I found myself looking at dresses in my closet the way you look at pictures of your first love—with a mix of nostalgia and yearning. Going to a restaurant after months of hiding from a deadly virus definitely felt like an occasion. I hesitantly put on something pretty and flouncy I hadn't worn in ages, having shoved it to the back of the rack to make room for my jumpsuits long before COVID was a thing. Lo and behold, it actually fit (or close enough? Not like a glove exactly, but like a reliable mitten). Encouraged, I put on a shoe with a little heel. I stood in front of the mirror, almost in shock at seeing this version of me still there. I felt like I was looking at some woman I used to know, like a college friend who maybe wasn't on social media and you thought perhaps had died, but then one day you run into them at the supermarket and you just can't believe it, and while they're talking you pretend you're listening but really you're just in wonder at how their face flickers, like a light, between the present and the past, the person in front of you and the person you used to know.

The Car Seat

"Once having traversed the threshold, the hero . . .
must survive a succession of trials."

—Joseph Campbell

I am standing in a playground parking lot, trying to get Asher into his car seat. He is three, so he is old enough to climb in on his own, but he's also young enough to be whining the entire time. It's eleven a.m., and it's already ninety-seven degrees. He is melting down, literally and figuratively, as am I. We need to get home, where there is more lunch and less park, because we are DONE with that now. The more he whimpers, the more panic I feel to rush, and the more I rush, the more he whimpers. Even with all the doors open, the car feels like an oven. Asher keeps squirming; the buckle that goes over his crotch is stuck under his butt. "Lift your tush," I say. He tries but can't because the chest straps are too tight, so then I have to loosen the chest harness by pressing on a hidden metal lever, during which time he kicks his shoes off and one falls out of the car. I have pulled the straps from behind his shoulders that click down into the crotch piece, but then notice, with panic creeping up my throat and sweat rolling down my tits, that one of the straps is completely twisted right where it threads through the metal guide. I start trying to straighten the strap through the metal, but the opening is a centimeter wide and it won't budge. Everyone who has ever been taught how to buckle the car seat correctly knows it's a sin to move the vehicle with the straps twisted. I try again. Asher is yelling, "MOM! STOP!" and right about then is when I step away from the car, take a deep breath to collect myself, and yell, "FUCK! FUCK! FUCK!" at the top of my lungs. People are looking at me. Asher is looking at me. I am not meant to be doing this. I am meant to be doing something else. I am meant to be drinking with a girlfriend, talking some fun shit about someone we know. I am meant to be writing little satiric comments on the internet, or staring absentmindedly out a window, or lightly exercising. I do not have the capacity for the level of anxiety that comes with potentially getting this wrong. And yet . . . we have to get the fuck out of here.

We are so blessed to live at a time when we have car seats to help keep our children safe while driving. Nevertheless, I hate car seats.* There are a million consumer reports about what car

---

* How many times throughout this book do I need to say I'm grateful for or love something before I'm allowed to complain about it? I'm feeling like maybe four times. This might be the last. I personally believe a little complaining is good for you.

seat is best and user ratings and safety ratings, but there is no rating based on how batshit every single one of them will make you, which I guess makes sense because truthfully every single one of them will, so why bother quantifying it?

I realize some people reading this book may not be parents, so I'll frame it this way: imagine that every time you want to leave the house, you have to get into a bar fight with someone: a sloppy, exhausted, poorly choreographed display of slapping and kicking. You are in a bar fight because they don't want to be strapped, Hannibal Lecter–style, into the back of your car. (Fair.) Even though you are technically big enough to always win the fight, you still have to buckle a small (but shockingly heavy) person at a forty-five-degree angle, possibly in the burning sun or freezing cold or driving rain, into a chair, all the while vaguely recalling the warning that if the buckles are not in the exact right place then the whole point of putting them in the seat is moot and you've ruined everything. If the straps are not tight enough, or if they are too tight—you might as well just throw your kid on the roof of the car untethered to anything and drive off at a million miles per hour because it's all basically the same effect.

The other thing no one will tell you is how deeply, and for how long, not just you, but also your child, will hate the car seat. They will resist it and scream about it and say that you're hurting them and IT HURTS SO MUCH. One of the things that has continuously amazed me about my son is the paradox of how much he seems to love life versus how much he loathes so many of the basic things we must do to keep him alive. He will not eat a vegetable, or really, anything besides bread and cheese.* He loathes going to sleep. He loathes following directions when we're outside. He loathes putting on weather-appropriate clothes. But for a long time, really, what he hated most of all was getting strapped into the car seat.

Car seats are a relatively new invention. I grew up in New York City, so we didn't have a car, but my suburban friends report that they would just get tossed into the back of a station wagon and everyone would hope for the best. People weren't even coming to full stops to let their kids get in and out. I know people loved and cared about their kids just as much as we do now, but there were fewer legally enforceable ways you had to show it. The scope of how and when to worry seemed at least a little bit smaller, even though the dangers were similar.

When I was four years old, I decided to see if the door to our apartment, which was on the top floor of a six-story walk-up building, was unlocked. Lo and behold, it was. The next flight up from us was the roof entry, which was also unlocked. The wall that ran around the roof's edge, separating anyone who went up there from a seven-flight drop into oblivion, was three and a half feet high at best, and sloped. Honestly, thinking about it now makes me so dizzy I need to stop typing and lie on the floor for a moment. The roof wasn't really designed to be a place for hanging out; it was just an unadorned tar surface, but because it was New York City in the '70s, everyone hung out

---

* At least this makes sense. I mean, it's what I too truly want.

everywhere. My parents would occasionally take us up there, especially in the summer. My mom would snake a garden hose over the side of the building to our kitchen window one floor down, where my dad would hook it up to our faucet, turning the hose on the roof into our own sprinkler.

Maybe I was thinking of the sprinkler as I headed onto the roof. Maybe I was remembering some fun and was wondering if it was still happening? I don't know. I just remember I was alone. I remember looking at the sky and how big and open it was. I remember I could see the World Trade Center on one side and the Empire State Building on the other. It was a beautiful view. An unspecified amount of time later, my mom realized I was gone, saw the open door, and for some reason thought to come running up the stairs, where she found her child toddling inexplicably toward the edge of the roof.

The point is, my parents had not installed a childproof knob on our apartment door. They hadn't installed one because one didn't exist, and yet, they didn't wring their hands over its lack of existence. They simply assumed that things would be fine, which I suppose, they mostly were. I survived, and grew up, and I got married, and I had a baby, and now I hate his car seat.

If just Asher hated it, or just I hated it, I would be okay, I think. But our mutual agitation alchemizes all too often into a mutual desire to avoid dealing with the seat altogether. This was especially true when he turned two and could talk. "I don't want to go out," he would say. I didn't know if he felt this way because he didn't want to deal with the seat, but I didn't want to go out either, and for me it was definitely the seat. But choosing to stay home all day because the process of getting in the car seemed overwhelming felt as insane as screaming "fuck" at the top of my lungs while strapping my kid into my car.

Ever since I became a mother, his safety and my sanity have had trouble existing at the same time. Obviously he must be safe. But is he truly safe if his mother doesn't feel sane? No. But can I ever feel sane if he is not completely safe?

No.

Ughhhhhhhhhhhhhhhhh.

A woman who went by the direct but not-very-creative name of the Car Seat Lady installed our seat before Asher was born. We found her on the internet when we realized that installing an infant car seat yourself is almost impossible, and she asked us to meet her on a random street corner, as if she were a drug dealer. She was soft-spoken and looked like a normal person, which is why it was so surprising when her lesson in car seating turned out to be so aggressively intense. She was extremely good at her job, which is to say she was soul-crushingly precise. The actual strapping of the seat into the car involved a wrench, a carpenter level, and multiple do-overs. She wanted to talk Mike through it so he would have the muscle memory of doing it. However, she was so militaristic about the specificity of the angle and the tightness of the bolting, it was as if she were verbally guiding someone on how to build a NASA shuttle that would actually have to bring astronauts safely into space. A vein in Mike's head started bulging. Since I was the pregnant one, I decided I had the right to zone out for this part and busied myself watching a squirrel in a nearby tree.

Once the base was installed, however, she took out one of those disturbingly lifelike medical-type baby dolls, the kind you learn CPR on, that she wanted us both to practice strapping into the seat. The two prime tools required to do this correctly are manual dexterity and patience, neither of which I possess. Now it is my turn to sweat. I try to do the Car Seat Lady's bidding, but she keeps correcting me: The chest harness has to be exactly nipple height. The straps have to be pulled about a thousand times tighter than you'd expect. The baby's head must be here, not a centimeter higher or lower, or everything will burst into flames. Every lever and metal fastener is hidden, and you have to put your foot down inside the car to properly brace your body to pull with enough heft. Since the seat has to be rear-facing, I ask her if we should get one of those little mirrors everyone puts on the back of the passenger seat so you can look at your child occasionally. I may as well have asked her if I should punch myself repeatedly in my pregnant stomach. "Absolutely not," Car Seat Lady says, her eyebrows lowering into a Shar-Pei-level furrow. She explains that in the instant you glance to peek at your baby, you could be hit by an oncoming car and then you will both be fucking killed. I look into the medical baby's little plastic eyes. It doesn't trust me. I don't trust me either.

Months later, we are at a newborn care class, and we meet another couple who also paid the Car Seat Lady for a lesson.

The husband tells us that as she was walking him through installing their seat, he reached under the left passenger side to secure a strap and saw something metal sticking out from under the driver's seat. He looked more closely and saw that, loose, on the floor of his car, was a meat cleaver. He then remembered he'd bought a knife set from West Elm a year prior and put it in the back of his car, and had only noticed upon arriving home that one piece was missing; he assumed it was a factory error. But it wasn't. A meat cleaver had fallen out of the box and had been rolling around in the back of his car for months. And now Car Seat Lady had seen it.

I think of this hero often.

In the month before Asher is born, I try to practice with the seat. I don't have a baby doll, so I use an old stuffed tiger I've had since I was eight. (His name is King, but that doesn't matter, he's extremely elegant, whatever.) A light dusting of crazy starts to blow through my brain as I step back to see if the stuffed tiger looks safely arranged. He does not. *What if I'm never a good mother?* I think to myself, only later realizing that a good mother would probably not consider a plush toy cat a proper stand-in for her own child's body during a dress rehearsal for motor vehicle safety.

With all of the anxiety surrounding having a baby for the first time, for some reason, my fear of the car seat loomed the largest.

Maybe this is because my muscle memory of being a child in New York City was that on the rare occasion when we had to be in a car, we were in a taxicab. It was the '80s, and there were no car seats. My father's anxiety on these occasions was palpable, and it manifested in him frequently demanding the driver stop the cab to let us out before the trip was complete. He'd angrily pay as we all awkwardly hopped out, the driver cursing us under his breath. Stranded on some random corner, like a family of ducks far from their pond, my father would hail another cab and we'd start all over. Sometimes it would take us two or three cabs just to travel a mile.

When I was thirty-two and took a job in LA, I finally had to get my license. I failed the driving test twice before a DMV employee took pity on me and overlooked several errors, I'm pretty sure because I was wearing a Mets hat and we both liked Mookie Wilson. At some point between test failure number one and successful try number three, I was venting to my dad about how wildly difficult attaining a license is and he told me he'd let his license lapse when my siblings and I were little— not just because we lived in Manhattan and didn't have or need a car, but because, he said, "I was too nervous to drive with you guys."

I often think about my father's anxiety around driving, which somehow made him both too nervous to drive us himself, and too nervous to let others do it. Maybe there's something genetic here; maybe I am predisposed to see getting into a car with my child as a fight-or-flight situation. And the car seat, which is supposed to make us feel safer, instead somehow makes this preexisting fear worse. Maybe because it puts the illusion of control back onto me. If I can strap my son correctly into the seat, we will be okay. But really, even if I take deep breaths and meditate my way through being screamed at by my own child, even if the Car Seat Lady were to give us Nadia Comaneci Car Seat Olympic Perfect Tens™, the truth is, I am never fully in control of what might happen to us. It's not really the car seat, then, that makes me crazy (although it does)—it's that the mental and physical gymnastics of putting in the seat aren't anywhere near as exhausting as the endless, day-in-day-out worry that the seat would only be enough if we could simultaneously strap down the entire world.

You cannot restrain the world, but sometimes I pass parents who have put that little yellow BABY ON BOARD sign in their window, which feels like an attempt. I'm a good citizen, so I always heed the sign and slow down. I don't want to be the asshole who fender bends a baby. And yet oddly, since becoming a mother, whenever I see that sign I can't help but think, Why isn't there a sign that just says ME ON BOARD? Because I am on board, and I feel more fragile than I ever have; certainly more fragile than I did when I was four, heading toward the edge of a seven-story rooftop but blissfully unaware that anything bad could happen. Because now I know that everything bad can happen, and I am responsible for it not. Because sometimes I feel like keeping us from dying will kill me. Because I am on board, and I'm exhausted. Because I am on board, and I will never be used to being the driver. I still feel like the baby; like I could just cry this whole ride and never stop till we get home.

An Open Love Letter to Nate Berkus and Jeremiah Brent

Hi, Nate Berkus and Jeremiah Brent. I'm torn between desperately hoping you will read this, which I know you never will, and praying that you won't, which you won't. So for whoever is reading this, which maybe includes Nate and/or Jeremiah—and I'm torn on if it was one of them who I would want to have read it more (Nate, probably, but gahhh, maybe Jeremiah!!)—here goes:

I am in love with Nate and Jeremiah. There, I've said it out loud, and now I feel better, because all I want to do ever is talk about Nate and Jeremiah and look at their Instagram feeds and watch their shows and look at their remodeled homes and read things that have been written by or about them and now I have freed myself to do this. I don't even know where to begin because I love everything about them. I guess the place to begin is with Nate, because I met him first.

Like the rest of America, I was introduced to Nate by our

mutual friend Oprah Winfrey. I'm going to get real vulnerable and say that Nate Berkus is the most handsome man I've ever seen in my life, and I say that as someone who did once see Clive Owen working out at a gym.* He has my favorite kind of face, which is to say, a meaty nose and chewy lips and a general warmth to his aura, a kind of lovely, sweet marzipan quality. I love his brond wavy hair and how it's always been perfect and has STAYED perfect, and then there is also something about his VOICE. Sigh, that voice. Nate always sounds like he's swallowing ice cream, which is exactly what I want a person to sound like if they're not in fact actually doing it for real. When he first appeared on *Oprah*, he would do makeovers on small spaces, which meant the world to me because I lived in a very small space and all I wanted was for this adorable man to come over and drape a string of beads over the corner of one of my mirrors, which I didn't even know was something a person could do! The first time he lifted the lid off a storage ottoman in a tiny apartment makeover I just about fainted. But

---

* Okay, so a few years ago I was lucky enough to be staying at the Four Seasons in LA for work and I went to the gym, mostly to see if there were any free bran muffins. I saw an extremely attractive man working out with a trainer—he sort of looked like a hot wolf standing on its hind legs. I realized the wolf was Clive Owen and immediately summoned all of my energy to hear every word of their conversation. They started talking about some special delivery meal system Clive was getting as part of prepping for a movie. The trainer asked how the diet was going, and I heard Clive say, in the politest, most British, and most human way possible, "The portions are a bit small?" This made me about as happy as anything ever has. Even Clive Owen thinks his portions should be bigger.

Nate taught me that kind of thing all the time. He was a dream gay husband.

Then Jeremiah came along and Nate actually married him, so now he had a real gay husband, and I'll admit I was hurt. Hurt and, dare I say it, skeptical. (Jeremiah, I am sorry but that's how I felt, and I am saying this in the spirit of acknowledging I am now someone who loves you TOO MUCH.) Who was this person, and what were his intentions with my Nate? Who was this YOUNGER man who had won Nate's heart and was suddenly appearing with him everywhere and seemingly draping beads over things with him? It just all seemed suspicious. He's too handsome, for starters. He looks like the star of a '50s musical, like the kind of tempting young sailor you used to see walking wide-eyed around Times Square during Fleet Week. Jeremiah is always outfitted in a pair of perfectly draped pleated pants, ever-so-slightly tight T-shirts, and a perfect loafer. He's also usually wearing the most tastefully curated stack of gold bracelets atop a perfect vintage watch, which makes me nuts because this is what I want to do, but whenever I put on a bracelet I instantly look like a pirate. Every beautiful ensemble is topped off by a rakish hat of some kind. A fedora? Maybe it's even a chapeau? I'm not actually sure what a chapeau is, but whatever it is, I'm pretty sure it's on Jeremiah's head. Unlike most men who wear hats, he is not hiding any baldness—on the contrary, his hair is a confidently mussed thick golden wave. I worried that everything about Jeremiah seemed, as they frequently say on *The Bachelor*, "too good to be true." I really didn't like that he was so much younger and fretted that he was glomming on to

Nate's star. I started a casual conversation about my concerns with another Nate aficionado I know. Where did this guy *come from*, I asked? She informed me that she had seen him before on the short-lived reality show *The Rachel Zoe Project*, a worrying detail I could not accept. I know this is snobby to say, but that felt like a shoddy origin story. (Who am I to speak poorly of Rachel Zoe when I wolfed down *Love Island* like a fucking sleeve of Fig Newtons just a few weeks ago? That said, I wasn't IN it.*) I'm only able to write these terrible words about my new best friend Jeremiah now because he himself confessed in a podcast interview, one that I obsessively listened to twice last month while driving to work, that when he and Nate first started dating, "everybody thought I was a prostitute." HIS WORDS!

So, no, I was not thrilled about Nate and Jeremiah. I felt protective of Nate and couldn't stand the thought of him finding anything but the purest and most sacred love, which surely should only come in the shape of a best friendship with me. Even after they had a beautiful baby, I still just felt nervous that I did not really KNOW Jeremiah, and who knew what he might be up to at any moment in that hat with those bracelets?

But then in 2017, they made a TV show called *Nate & Jeremiah by Design*, where they helped people deal with stalled home renovations—or something like that? I can't remember what it was about exactly because for me it was about watching

---

* That said, would be there in a heartbeat if asked.

THEM. Their body language. I have never seen two people more in love. The way Nate casually flings his arm over Jeremiah's shoulders. The way Jeremiah reflexively rests his hand on Nate's knee. The way Jeremiah lovingly teases Nate and the way Nate teases back and no one gets overly mad or silently mopey the way some people writing this book and their husband possibly do. I began to fall for Jeremiah. Nate is still physically more my type, but as the season progressed, I will confess, I felt like I emotionally related to Jeremiah more, if that makes sense? Even though they are both deeply compassionate toward the people they are helping, people who have truly done some spectacularly insane bad things to their homes, Jeremiah is the MOST compassionate. Like Nate, he also has an amazing voice—but whereas Nate's is deep and ice-cream-y, Jeremiah's is more mischievous, playful but calm, best friend meets meditation app. There are so many moments in the show where Nate is talking and Jeremiah gazes at him adoringly and then Jeremiah turns to talk to the camera and the way Nate looks at him, lids slightly lowering over loving blue eyes, you just ... I know it's a cliché, but find you a man who looks at you the way Nate and Jeremiah look at Nate and Jeremiah.

I watched every episode of this show. I watched them fill homes with weathered vases and antique bowls, little sculptures, dining room banquettes. They knocked out walls and opened up windows. They pulled up carpets and put down little kilim rugs. They threw ugly flush-mount light fixtures in the fucking trash and replaced them with Spanish chandeliers. Every now and then we would get a delicious peek into a slice of their home life, their life as parents of an adorable girl and then a beautiful boy, their life as a couple out having fun dinners with friends. But you could feel the emotional balance of their marriage no matter what they were doing. They made doorways twice the size of regular doorways. They filled horrific, dank bathrooms with claw-foot tubs, creating a perfect little oasis that was almost always topped off with a little succulent plant on the back of the toilet tank. That always got me. As soon as I see a succulent, I forget I'm looking at a toilet. How do they know all these tricks?

My one annoyance with the show was that for (one assumes) budgetary reasons, they would only renovate part of the home. Like the living room and the kitchen would be perfect, but then the show apparently didn't have the money to finish the whole house, so every other room of the house would still be a bedraggled mess. Each episode would leave me in a slightly blue-balled state, wanting them to fix it, to fix everything, to come through the screen and drape beads over me.

Nate and Jeremiah had moved to LA from New York City with their little daughter right around the time we did. They renovated a twelve-million-dollar Hancock Park home and suffice to say they didn't need to worry about dressing up a toilet with a plant. They would usually begin their show sitting on the couch in their enormous but tastefully understated living room. I liked knowing we lived close to each other just in case we suddenly became friends and they wanted me to come over. Not to brag, but I did drive by the supermarket one afternoon and saw them sitting outside with their daughter and I lightly vibrated for the rest of the day.

Aside from the voyeuristic pleasure of their marble countertops, their hair, and their casual intimacy, it also felt comforting to me that in a world where they had the means to live absolutely anywhere, they had chosen to live in the same city as me, a city that, to be honest, I do not really like. I am sorry, Los Angeles. But the truth is I have never quite felt at home here. I long for New York City and walking everywhere and seeing a million weirdos a minute as soon as I step out to get coffee.

Underlying my borderline creepy interest in Nate and Jeremiah was—is—my pervasive homesickness. Homesickness has been a problem for me since I was a child; a chronic condition, like asthma, that has ebbed and flowed better or worse from year to year. As a kid I could never make it all the way through a sleepover; I would last till about eleven p.m., when a specific sense of anxiety that I was in the wrong place would come over me, and then, after an awkward conversation with the host friend's mom, I'd have to call my parents, through light tears, to come get me. I was embarrassed and would try to fight it, but I almost always succumbed to that sinking sensation of something feeling askew in my heart. It was like a little bird-cry coming from within, yelling out that for some reason she feels she's fallen out of the right nest. But once I grew into an adult, it all became more complicated. Now when I get the homesick feeling, the only person who can come pick me up is me. I yell at the bird to shut the fuck up because aren't we (the bird and I) lucky and privileged to have a roof over our heads at all, and the answer, of course, is a resounding yes.

But homesickness isn't about houses; it's about that elusive sense of something else, of peace and calm and happiness and belonging and relaxation that all at some point etymologically swirled into that other word over the years: "home," which is etymologically perhaps related to the Irish *"coim,"* meaning "pleasing or pleasant."

When Nate and Jeremiah's show premiered my boy was two, and our house was a swirl of plastic toys and blocks and really ugly beeping things and Aquaphor. It was not *coim.* My marriage was not *coim.* As a mother I never felt *coim.* I try not to yell, but I yell all the time. Nothing ever felt *coim.* What did feel *coim* was: watching Nate and Jeremiah on basic cable while eating takeout balanced on my lap after my child went to bed; following Nate and Jeremiah on Instagram; and following everyone they followed so that at night, unable to sleep, I could scroll through an endless feed of other people's beautifully arranged homes. Some of them were fancy, some of them were small and humble, but all of them pulsed with *coim.* I would emotionally project myself into these little Instagram squares, imagining myself sitting on some bouclé-covered couch in a cozy Parisian flat, or curled up next to a fireplace in some hygge little A-frame cabin in Norway.

Then one day, in the middle of season three of *Nate & Jeremiah by Design,* something happened. Nate and Jeremiah were on a family hike in Runyon Canyon (I was eating ice cream while I watched them climb a mountain). Looking out over the view of the canyon, Nate turned to Jeremiah and said: "What about this? How do you feel when you look at all this?" I perked up. What was this question? What was really being asked? How does Jeremiah feel when he looks at WHAT?

They teased us for another episode before the big reveal. Which was: THEY WERE MOVING BACK TO NEW YORK. Jeremiah wanted to move back there, and even though Nate seemed fine with living in LA, that's what they were doing. Jeremiah missed the energy of the city and wanted his kids to grow up seeing lots of different kinds of people all the time. They immediately began showing clips of them looking at town houses in the Village—MY NEIGHBORHOOD, IN MY HOMETOWN—as if we didn't need time to ABSORB this information, to process what was actually happening before they closed on a new home and got on a plane. I was in shock. I couldn't believe they were leaving me here!

It is embarrassing to admit how truly and deeply betrayed I felt by these two people I did not know.

A few weeks before I sat down to write this essay, *Architectural Digest* published a photo spread of Jeremiah and Nate's* newly renovated West Village town house. They both posted the link on their Instas at the same time because couples in love know to coordinate their socials! I clicked on the link to the pictures of this home at, I would say, approximately the speed of

---

* Switching the order of their names just for fun.

light? I looked at them for a long time, and then I put my phone down and tried to do work but came back and stared at them again. What is there to say? It's perfection. I so badly wanted to jump into my screen and slip down a magical slide directly to the couch in front of their wall of built-ins. I wanted to get on a plane and move my life back with them. I wanted us to watch a movie in their family room and for me to come over with wine and cheese but of course be the only one eating because they are both in incredible shape.

When I think back to the earliest years of motherhood, when my baby was one and two and three years old, my sense memory is primarily of sitting in an endless series of messes. On the floor, sopping up various baby body fluids with wipes, and then when I ran out of wipes, using my sleeves or my pants. I spent countless hours at a baby gym class, literally a giant padded room, sitting on a blue rubber floor with my toddler while throwing rainbow scarves in the air. (He was supposed to throw them, but he wouldn't, so I did it for him.) I spent countless hours on the floor in our house picking up toys, and then lying on the floor next to his crib until he fell asleep, using a stuffed elephant as a pillow. On the floor, wiping up errant pee. In these moments, it's impossible for your mind not to wander elsewhere, not to want to go some other place that isn't filled with pee and poop and plastic and padded toddler gymnastics wedges. For some it might be a memory of a place they've been, a vacation that's been taken, or a vacation that hasn't been taken but, fuck, maybe one day when the baby is grown-up. For me,

I want to go to Nate and Jeremiah's house, where everything is arranged in perfect harmony.

Nate and Jeremiah, if you're reading this (and it can't be overstated how much I know you're not, and I do think that's for the best), I'm sorry that I was ever angry with you. The longer I sat with it, the more I realized my anger was, in fact, a yearning jealousy.

They seemed, as a unit, to be the very embodiment of *coim*, with each other, their gorgeous surroundings, their sweet family, their TV show, and their perfectly curated accessories. But really the most *coim* thing about them was the fact that the whole time I'd been watching them on TV, Jeremiah had been feeling that I-want-someone-to-come-and-pick-me-up feeling, and Nate answered the call.

Sigh and swoon.

Underwear Sandwich

There are so many things no one tells you about birth (and afterbirth). You hear tidbits, rumors, little whispers that don't seem to have a nameable, reliable source. It's a shame that, after approximately one billion years of giving birth, women still have to rely on a makeshift underground network of gossip to know what is going to happen to them when they push out a baby.

A few hours after my labor, my son was taken to the nursery while my epidural wore off and I recovered. At around ten p.m., a nurse—an old-school type who I think was named Francine? Or maybe she just seemed like a Francine—came to see if I was ready to stand on my feet. Once we established that I could support my own weight, she took out my catheter (yum) and helped me walk to the bathroom. That's when she said:

"So, before you can try to pee or poop on your own, you've gotta learn how to make an underwear sandwich."

What?

She continued:

"Everything is gonna be a little sore and different down there, so for a couple weeks, whenever you gotta go, you're gonna have to make an underwear sandwich."

Something about those two words together felt like a bucket of ice water being poured over my head. They were a shock.

Underwear. Sandwich.

The closest these words had ever come, in my previous life experience, was maybe being on the same to-do list: *Call grandma. Buy new underwear. Make sandwich.* But that's being generous. In truth, I've made a lot of lists, and I know that wasn't one of them. The point is, I'm certain that in my entire life's history of speaking thoughts aloud, these two words have never been adjacent.

The nurse went on to explain (I'm paraphrasing) that the base of the sandwich is disposable mesh underwear; I suppose you could refer to the disposable mesh underwear as the "bread." Next comes a maxi pad the size of a small baguette. I realize I'm confusing things by using a bread comparison for something that is already going on top of metaphorical bread, but I dunno, maybe think of it as the meat? No matter how you slice it, the entire sandwich is gross—I don't know what to tell you, I'm sorry. The "lettuce" is a gel ice pad out of the freezer, the kind of thing a professional soccer player might use to soothe an injured shin, except it's not for a soccer player's shin, it's for a woman's entire perineum. You have to balance the ice pad as best as you can on top of the enormous maxi pad. Then (yeah gurl, this isn't over) on top of the ice pad, you have to line up a few circular witch hazel pads like little pepperonis, and finally, the last thing you need is a plastic squeezie bottle* filled with lukewarm water (so basically the oil and vinegar thingy), which they tell you to squirt up into (what remains of) your vagina after you attempt to expel anything from yourself, because trying to use toilet paper would be like dragging a cheese grater across your tongue.

Now, I know what you're wondering: What's the top slice of bread on the sandwich? The answer: There isn't one? Unless you count your vulva? Or you could think of it as an open-faced sandwich, one that has to be remade about every two hours. Also, you have to refill your squeezie bottle with new lukewarm water every time you need to pee or poop.

At first I didn't understand why this was all necessary. It seemed like an awful lot of underwear sandwich for not a huge amount of problem? The reason I thought this was because my epidural hadn't fully worn off. The first time I actually peed with the medication completely out of my system, I almost cried. That's before I had to poop. Before I go on, I'm going to give you a trigger warning so you can bail on what's coming if you'd like. I'm not even sure how to describe the trigger; maybe trigger warning for HARD TRUTHS?

Anyway, it took a day or two before I could get up the

---

* The bottle the nurse gave me immediately reminded me of the one filled with oil and vinegar they had behind the counter at Blimpie, a place where, while working a temp job in my early twenties, I ate a fried chicken patty sandwich every single day for three straight months.

courage to try. They won't let you leave the hospital until you've had a bowel movement, and I did not want to live there, so it seemed best to make it happen. I remember feeling like I had to poop. I shuffled to the bathroom with my squeezie bottle. I started to try to push—but then . . . hmm, how to say . . . there was nothing to push. It felt like my poop just sort of . . . fell out. Because—and there's really no other way I can think to describe this—there was nothing to push against. My butthole (and I'm sorry, I do think that's the best choice available to me; I will not say "anus"), I guess, was so . . . spent? . . . that there was no feeling of stretching or resistance. I couldn't imagine how it looked down there and actually didn't want to know. This is when I actually started to cry, tears rolling as I squeezied warm water into myself and then began the process of making my underwear sandwich. Was I stuck this way? Had my genitals been permanently altered? My hormones were obviously going haywire, which did not make for clearheaded thinking, and, adding insult to injury, my witch hazel pepperonis kept falling off my giant ice pad.

I can't help but hypothesize that I might have felt better if someone, anyone, had told me in advance about the underwear sandwich. But nobody had. Nobody had even told me about the concept of the underwear sandwich without using the term "underwear sandwich," which I recognize might have been specific to Francine.

Why is this? I mean, I'd been pregnant for nine months. Someone could have brought it up, right?

But while we're at it, why should you have to be pregnant

to learn about this aspect of life? Why isn't this something everyone is told about? I suppose you might say because it's not relevant to them, but if we were to go by this measuring stick, I'm certain most of us would only know about forks and microwaves.

As it is, we in fact do learn a lot about bodies and puberty as we go through school.

However, even though I never heard a whisper about the brass tack details of what happens to the female body during and after birth, I know for certain I was taught MULTIPLE times over, in different health classes throughout NYC public junior high and high school, that boys have "nocturnal emissions" (also known as "wet dreams," a term that, if I'm being honest, feels ick to type, but at least I'm not the one who made it up?). But why did I need to know this? Why did I, a teenage girl, need to be instructed REPEATEDLY that teenage boys have fantastically vivid sex dreams that end with them jizzing in their sheets . . . and yet none of us needed to learn about the details of birth that bring us into this world? Why is so much of this knowledge made to feel like a dirty secret that can only be unearthed at the exact moment it's needed? Is it so unspeakable? Why did my lovely mother-in-law, who came to help us after the baby was born, feel she had to try to discreetly slip me the large CVS bag filled with my postpartum care requests ("all of the largest pads in the store")? The pads were so enormous she may as well have tried to discreetly slip me an air fryer. And yet, still, she tried to hand me the bag without my husband seeing—as if he were not aware that I was BLEEDING

OUT. Meanwhile, she'd had to wander around the store to find all of the underwear sandwich ingredients. Why aren't these available to purchase as one bundled kit at every drugstore on Earth?

I want to give credit where credit is due here and say that while writing this chapter, I googled to see if anyone was doing this and found that the baby product company Frida does sell a bundled underwear sandwich (although again, not under that name, which does feel like a missed opportunity). Impressed by the fact that they were making an effort to fill the underwear sandwich niche, I went to the "about" section of their website, which read as follows:

> "Mom's everyday toolkit: AKA the secret tools you rave about, blog about and share with other parents just like you."

WHY ARE THE TOOLS "SECRET"? Why does a company whose profit depends on publicity, in its own marketing, still have to perpetuate the idea that its products must exist in secrecy. WHY?

I don't have the answer to any of the aforementioned whys. All I know is, that moment in the hospital just continues to linger with me: sitting under fluorescent lights on the toilet trying to follow the nurse's directions, fumbling with bottles, pads, ice, and witch-hazel circles while bleeding, scared, and exhausted; and I think about all of the women all over the world in this same vulnerable position, and how someone should have told us about all of this.

And I just can't get it out of my head that I learned so many times about wet dreams, and never about underwear sandwiches. It was clearly so important to the curriculum, and to pop culture at large, that boys be prepared for those exciting messy dreams; the remains of which are so frequently laundered away, without a word, by their mothers.

My Future Lesbian Wife

Every now and then, I fantasize about my future lesbian wife. I'm not saying I want to get divorced, and I'm not saying I'm gay. I'm just saying, in about ten years or so, IF, by some small chance, I'm not still living a straight, married life, I'll probably (hopefully?) be living with a wife. I spend a few minutes a week thinking about this next (possible) chapter of (who knows—maybe?) my life.

Sexuality is obviously a spectrum, and I'm not saying divorced women who end up with wives were Once Straight but have now Turned Gay. I do believe most people are probably at least a teensy smidge fluid while some are fully liquid? And I just think I've been noticing in the last few years what I'd conservatively call an uptick in the number of women I've known who were married to men, had a kid or two, got divorced just as they were considered women of a certain age,* and upon reentering the dating world, suddenly realized they were, sometimes to their own great surprise, no longer interested in chasing that D.† These friends met other ladies who were nice to them and thought they were hot even though they no longer looked nineteen years old, and then they hooked up and thought, *OH WAIT YES THIS FEELS PRETTY NICE.* And they ended up in gay relationships and suddenly were, as the kids say, happy AF. I'm pretty sure this could be me. Again, I'm just saying, I'm not not thinking about it.

But this is kind of new for me. I'm not one of those ladies of the '90s who of course had a girlfriend my sophomore year of college, even though I went to Vassar, where by far the queerest thing you could do was be straight all the time. Here is a brief history of my gay experience, as of this writing, age forty-two:‡

To begin, I grew up in Greenwich Village and at my elementary school, a lot of our teachers were gay. Because it was public school in Greenwich Village in the early '80s, all of the women in this milieu, regardless of their sexuality, shared a similar aesthetic (thrift-store clothes, no makeup, all possessions carried in a constant jumble of assorted PBS pledge drive tote bags, and, I'm assuming, huge pubic bushes all around). I recognize this was not a "gay experience" per se so much as

---

* This fucking phrase. I mean honestly I would rather just be called a million years old.
† Dick.
‡ Jesus Christ.

it was an experience of just being around gay people, I'm just saying that with the lesbian teachers and the straight moms all carrying the same canvas tote bag, it was hard, as a child, to get obsessed with labels.

In college, I made it through most of my four years without having sex with anyone, let alone a woman. I did receive one awkward backrub from a female friend, during which I thought maybe, just maybe she was trying to touch the side of my boob a little bit? For which I was grateful. I remember that as she massaged me, I went back and forth in my head about whether I'd go along with it if she started to actually make out with me, and right as I decided I would, the backrub ended and we went back to listening to Liz Phair. I was disappointed.

But the fact that I wasn't having lesbian sex didn't seem to make a difference in how I was perceived, as I found out when I finally began dating my college boyfriend late in my junior year. He was friendly with the cool hipster alpha girls I'd lived next door to the entire year prior. They were the kind of girls who, even though they'd only be living in their dorm room for ten months, had tricked it out with enough gorgeous vintage furniture that it basically looked like the set of Sofia Coppola's *Marie Antoinette*. These girls barely ever spoke to me. They were nice enough when we passed each other in the hall, but essentially I was like a bespectacled little nerd ghost they occasionally walked through on their way to and from parties that might as well have been taking place on Pluto as far as I was concerned. When Pete and I finally got together, he told me that he'd asked them whether I was single at least a year before our first date and they'd said, without an ounce of hesitation, "Yeah, but she's gay." Nevertheless, #hepersisted.

In my early thirties, I moved part-time to LA for my first TV writing job. Because I was keeping my apartment in New York and wouldn't be moving all my stuff west, I had to find furnished sublets, which led to me living in a series of guesthouses, which, totally by chance, were all lesbian-owned. One of them was a small but magical little studio set behind a gorgeous craftsman house inhabited by two women, Susan and May, and their young son from Susan's previous marriage to a man. They had two dogs and a cat and lovely taste. Their house was filled with orchids and the kind of oversized comfortable pillows you'd have to go to court to keep if you tried to put them in a house you shared with a straight dude. I never heard them fight as I typed away in the back, staring up occasionally at the large, glittering Balinese goddess statue that serenely surveyed the room from her perch atop a gorgeous built-in salvaged shelf. This same statue looked peacefully at me as my New York boyfriend broke up with me over the phone, and I remember sobbing into a deliciously big pillow as I looked longingly toward the main house and wondered how much happier Susan was now than before. I wondered if she had always known she was gay but couldn't come out so she got married, or if she had loved her husband and not thought at all about women until after she was divorced, or if she hadn't thought about women for even a second until she met May specifically? Despite this bummer of a setback in my heterosexual relationship, I continued attempting to date men, and a few years later I met Mike and we got engaged and it seemed like I was committing forever to a straight path.

Three weeks before our wedding, however, we got into an absolutely enormous fight. I have no memory whatsoever of what it was about, but it felt huge enough that we might need to call the whole thing off. I stormed out of our apartment and promptly realized I was standing in the middle of a NYC street with no fucking place to go. I called all my friends to see if anyone could grab a drink, but everyone was either genuinely busy, or completely available but for some reason not seduced by my sniffly, self-pitying voicemails. I found myself walking around my neighborhood of birth, the Village, where in times of trouble I always return, like a salmon.

So I'm walking around, fuming about my relationship but also with every passing minute having the panicky realization that if I bail on getting married, I'm now in a real pickle because I've already given up my old apartment* and it's starting to rain. Maybe this is why people get married, to have a place to be when it's raining. As my jacket begins to soak, I notice that *Blue Is the Warmest Color* is playing at the IFC theater on Sixth Avenue and West Third. I don't know much about it except it's about a lesbian relationship and it's about four hours long and I guess maybe I heard something about sex scenes? All of this

---

* This is not in any way an advice book, but I must give any young women reading this a piece of advice: Never give up your apartment. Never, ever, ever give it up. Sublet it illegally until you're taken to prison; it is worth it.

sounds enticing, but especially the four hours part seeing as how I can't go home because I'm so mad at my straight male fiancé. So in I go to watch the film alone. Somehow even though I wasn't wearing a trench coat I felt like I was wearing a trench coat?

In case you haven't seen the movie, I won't spoil it except to say if you are looking to be simultaneously the horniest and most emotionally decimated you've ever been in your life, then run, don't walk, to see *Blue Is the Warmest Color* by yourself in a theater on a rainy day. Or, if that's not possible, just do what I've done and download it to your laptop so you can endlessly replay the naughty parts, because holy shit. There are three or four sex scenes that are each about ten minutes long and shot in real time, and these women are both the hottest people you've ever seen but in, like, unreplicable, unique ways, and truly I might have to take a break just thinking about it.

Okay, I'm back.

Walking out of the movie and heading home to see the boyfriend I wanted to murder, I started to seriously ponder the notion, for the first time in my life, that maybe I could one day retire from straightness and start a new gay chapter. It's like how for the kind of people who have lived their whole lives in New York City and can't possibly picture ever living anywhere else, they one day finally visit Portland and think, *Ohhhhh, I could see myself living in Portland!* Maybe the salmon doesn't have to always go back to Greenwich Village. Maybe the salmon can go live with her future lesbian wife somewhere else.

I find myself constructing a somewhat elaborate fantasy

about how I might meet this woman. In the fantasy, she is a ceramics teacher. I've just finished up a terrible date with a guy from some app who'd convinced me on text he was an artsy, funny, sensitive type, but as soon as we meet up, it becomes clear he's a dud. I struggle through one drink and then can't take it anymore and just end the date. It's raining and I don't have an umbrella and just as it starts to really pour I happen to walk by a storefront ceramics studio where a few people are taking a class. The instructor (my future wife) happens to see me and waves me in. I apologize for interrupting, but she invites me to pull up a chair and play around with some clay; one of the students had to cancel so there's an extra space. (Yes, in my fantasy there's a ceramics class cancellation—can you even stand this heat?????????)

Anyway, in this scenario, my future lesbian wife is a couple of years older than me. I picture her looking like Annette Bening, ruggedly beautiful in her completely natural aging process and wearing an old-school jumpsuit, like the kind you see in Edward Hopper paintings of gas stations.* She hands me a glass of wine and shows me how to make a mug handle. I get buzzed and make a better-than-expected mug and end up enrolling in a twelve-week class. She has the warmth and easy manner of

---

* Bening actually wore this outfit in Mike Mills's *20th Century Women*, and when I saw her wearing it I almost died from happiness as I realized this is what I want to wear and look like for the rest of my life. Just google "Annette Bening 20th Century Women jumpsuit." YOU'RE WEL-COME.

Meryl Streep. (I'm aware that in this fantasy my future lesbian wife is basically a mash-up of A-list actresses over forty-five.) Over the course of the semester, I realize that I feel more comfortable and happier around her than I have ever felt around anyone in my whole life, and finally, as we are saying goodbye on our last day of class and she's wrapping my Edo-period-inspired salad bowl in paper to take home, I start writing the speech in my head of what I'm going to say to her as soon as the moment comes to actually say goodbye. Then when that moment arrives she takes my face in her hands and kisses me and basically we start living together. We don't have to get into a whole game of cat and mouse because both of us, spiritually, are dog people.

We would live in Topanga Canyon, a place I've never been to but picture being chockablock with new lesbian wives. Our house is a modest boho cabin off a dirt road filled with the requisite big pillows and throwbeds and every floral teacup I ever wanted from a flea market that I didn't buy because I knew it'd bum my husband out. Everywhere there are rustic metal wind chimes, and somehow they always magically clink around at the exact moment of our sexual climaxes. We wake up in dappled sun patches and pour each other coffee into the beautiful wabi-sabi mugs my wife sells to abc carpet & home and a few hidden-gem boutiques around Northern California. When we're not in jumpsuits, we wear caftans all day.

I realize that my future lesbian wife fantasy is just that: a fantasy. It's all too easy, during the uphill marathon that is parenting a young child, to project all kinds of grass-is-greener feelings onto other lives, other places, other people, and even other sexualities? And at this time, when so much energy is being expended on caring for a little person who needs so much, who wouldn't dream of being nurtured and cared for just a touch more? THAT SAID: I do feel I must point out, accepting that perhaps I am wrong on this but I don't think I am, that there just doesn't seem to be an equivalent male phenomenon wherein a notable portion of men in their fifties, post divorce, just get on Grindr and end up with a dude. I know we women aren't perfect and fer sure we take energy to be in a relationship with, OF COURSE. Of course.

But I'm just saying, maybe the undeniable truth is, life is easier with a wife.

Listening to Beyoncé in the Parking Lot of Party City

On April 23, 2016, Beyoncé drops *Lemonade* at midnight. I cannot stop listening to *Lemonade*. Everyone's mind is blown, and it's all anyone is talking about because it's a masterpiece. Beyoncé is a genius. What do you do when life gives you *Lemonade*? You listen to it a million fucking times.

And that is what I do as I'm driving around town, clutching the steering wheel of my walnut-brown Prius, a bit too tight usually. I am either racing to work, or racing home from work to get to my child before the nanny must depart. When I get home I will feed Asher, stuff some food into my mouth over the sink while Mike bathes him, then go read to Asher before desperately trying to get him to go to sleep. When this is all over, I will have just enough time to try to write for an hour and fail, before I have to go to bed so I have enough energy to wake up with my son when he starts crying in the middle of the night. I increasingly find that if I step back and examine what emotion is simmering under my jittery, tight posture, it's looking more and more similar to rage? Or at least . . . something rage-esque? A frustration on steroids, compounding day after day. A feeling of *I can't keep doing this*, multiplied by doing it over and over.

I listen to "Hold Up" on repeat. I love it in that way you occasionally love a song that feels somehow it's coming from inside of you and outside of you at the same time. The opening notes are plodding, like the hooves of a clopping horse, then an airhorn . . . and then, Beyoncé's here.

Something don't feel right
Because it ain't right

About a month after *Lemonade* comes out, Mike and I start discussing how to celebrate our son's birthday. It feels like a miracle, that he is almost ONE and we all survived. I don't want to do a big event because when I say we survived, I feel like I'm definitively alive, but barelyish. I'm fatigued, I'm twenty-five pounds overweight, and having recently moved across the country, I don't have a sense of my bearings; I constantly feel like I'm on a leaky raft in open water.

Mike continues to stress that we need to do something to give the day a sense of occasion.

"Well, of course," I keep saying. "I'm not saying let's do nothing."

We continue to go in circles, and the vibe grows more and

more tense. But truthfully, it was already tense. Our almost-one-year-old's favorite wake-up time is four a.m. We are both working full-time and trying very hard to be good parents. We are exhausted. Like many couples in that first year after having a baby, we are in a bit of a dry spell.

Six weeks after I gave birth, I went for my checkup so that my doctor could "sign off" on me resuming sexual activity. She held up a little light and peeked into my vagina. "You look like you didn't even give birth," she said. This one hundred percent felt like a compliment, but at the same time I couldn't help but wonder, as Carrie Bradshaw often did, what your vagina looks like when it does look like you gave birth.

But the OB-GYN *Good Housekeeping* seal of approval can only go so far. Both parents have to reconstruct their sense of self after having a baby, and between my new body, my leaky boobs, and the lack of bedroom action, I am left feeling groove-less. Frustrated. I can't remember who I was before I was this person sitting awake in the middle of the night wearing a dirty breast-pumping bra, looking at Twitter while a machine sucks milk out of my nipples.

Or at least, I couldn't until *Lemonade.*

> *What's worse, lookin' jealous or crazy?*
> *Jealous or crazy?*

The song hit me like a tuning fork, eliciting a note that in the last two years I couldn't seem to produce on my own. It was a statement of sexual vitality in the face of anyone who would dare to deny it. It was Beyoncé, barefoot, a goddess in a chiffon yellow dress shattering car windows with a baseball bat, fueled by bright, hot anger while simultaneously looking like the coolest spring day.

One late afternoon, during my peak *Lemonade* obsession, I was driving home from work, listening to "Hold Up," and I was kind of feeling myself. The sun was setting, and the sky was glowing pink and orange. My windows were down so the warm late spring breeze could blow through. I was wearing my new sunglasses. This is embarrassing to admit but I'm a real asshole about thinking I'm more attractive in sunglasses. I stopped at a red light and another car pulled up to my right. I glanced over at the driver. With one tattooed arm dangling out his window, he was all white T-shirt and tan skin and scruff. He looked as if he'd been created from one of Ryan Gosling's ribs.

The red light at this particular intersection is a long one, so I had extra time to take him in. I was outright staring, with that false sense of security you get staring at people from your car. You always think they'll have no idea you're looking when in fact the most ESP humans ever have seems to be when someone is looking at them from another car. I was gawking at him quite freely when all of a sudden his head turned in my direction. My heart started to race. Holy shit. Was he staring at me?? Fuck, was he . . . in love with me? Between my cool sunglasses and Beyoncé blaring from my sound system, was my car enveloped in a cloud of pink pheromones? Was I like some red-assed baboon, my readiness to mate practically a flag waving in the air? I glanced back. He was still looking. I glanced away. Good Lord. I didn't want to cheat on my husband, and yet—here was this opportunity. All we had to do was pull over and then each open a door.

"Hey," he said.

Ohmigod, this is actually happening. I looked over. *Bye husband. Bye family. Bye life I know. Hello sunglasses me. Hello sexy new life with young boyfriend.*

"Hey there." *Be cool be cool be cool.*

"Hey."

He leaned out the window a bit.

"Can you tell me how to get to Hillhurst?"

He wanted directions. He did not want to kiss me or have sex with me or talk on the phone late into the night or any of the things that I had, for the length of a red light, imagined might be possible. The light turned green. The most intimacy we would ever achieve was the unspoken agreement that we would both ignore the traffic light until I'd finished telling him where to go. He made his left and I went straight, feeling horribly embarrassed. And as you do when you're horribly embarrassed, I suddenly became very interested in finding and naming everything about myself that was potentially ridiculous. This was how I remembered that I was driving around in a scratched-up walnut-brown*Prius with a child seat in the back, and that that child seat was covered with Cheerios and juice stains. There were balled-up Honest wipes on the floor, as well as some random sticks Asher and I had collected at the park. Somehow that Beyoncé feeling had made me momentarily forget that in terms of sexual magnetism I might as well have been driving an actual stroller. I think as a New Yorker who didn't get my license till my midthirties, I hadn't ever truly absorbed the fact that your car can be as much an expression of who you are as your clothes. I had forgotten that to anyone else's eyes, unlike the Wonder Woman version of me I had briefly fantasized into being—a beautiful, powerful woman driving an invisible vehicle—it was in fact me who was invisible, and my car that told whatever story there was to tell: Mom. Practical. Mess. Overwhelmed. Probably knows the way to Hillhurst.

A week later, I am wandering lost around the aisles of Party City. Mike and I have finally decided Asher's birthday will be an intimate affair, just a small group of friends and family at our house. Mike had advocated for some kind of entertainment, like a magician or a bubble artist.† I just could not justify paying for either when one-year-olds still barely even know where

---

* So the official color of my car is "walnut brown." But it isn't really the color of a walnut. To be clear, when I was looking at the car in the lot and deciding whether to buy it, I took a picture of it and texted it to my friend Kate. She wrote back, "Did not know prius makes a purple car?" So it's that kind of brown.

† I don't know what to tell you. There are bubble artists.

they are. (As I write this, Asher is four and still asks me every morning, "What day is it?") What I did think was essential, however, was helium balloons. It was the only party staple really capable of entertaining a twelve-month-old brain. And in all sincerity, part of me still finds helium balloons to be a very fancy extravagance and always will. When my siblings and I had birthdays as kids, we got the kind of balloons you blow up yourself, the rubber ones that come packed in a bag of a hundred, looking like sad little worms. On the rare occasions when a helium balloon made its way into the house, we would play with it long past its prime, until it was hovering by our heads, then our knees, then deceased on the ground, at which point we would continue to bat it around, like kittens playing with a dead mouse.

Since I was the one insisting on balloons, we agreed I would be the one in charge of getting them. This is why I find myself now, for the first time ever, cruising the kids' aisles at Party City. But as I said, I'm really more lost. I'm also supposed to be picking up napkins and plates and forks, but the number of choices feels overwhelming. The majority of what's here is garish merchandise from kids' shows I've never heard of. *Paw Patrol?* What the fuck is that? (It's only later that I will learn *Paw Patrol* is akin to *Seinfeld* in terms of popularity, and if you don't know about it you're basically a full idiot.)

I finally attach myself to the shockingly long line at the balloon order counter. While I wait, I look at the selections, so many questions arising. Mylar or rubber? One color or multi? Ten or twenty? How many balloons does it take for a room to feel festive? You don't want too many (gauche), but even worse is too few (cheap). Am I still attractive at all? I'm going to turn forty-one. How many more years do I have before I completely deflate? Should I get one of those numeral balloons? Those always feel fun. Is my vitality gone? Everything I am feeling seems to exist in complete opposition to the one billion aggressively upbeat details that create a Party City. A whole city made for partying. Still, when it is my turn to place my order, I do feel the happy anticipation of my boy getting this balloon bounty, as well as a rare glimmer of pride in myself for being, maybe, a decent mother, one who is so on top of things that I am even arranging to have the balloons ready for pickup the day before so I don't get stuck waiting on line as the celebration is about to begin, since we're scheduled to start at the very sexy hour of ten a.m.

So this is how I fucked up the balloons.

The day before the party, Mike and I are going over our checklist. He is in charge of catering, and because he is actually good at "accomplishing" "tasks," the house is already filled with juice boxes, and an armored truck's worth of mac and cheese is due to be delivered in the afternoon. Our standard tension is exacerbated by the nerves we're having about throwing a small birthday party for our baby. "Where are we on balloons?" he asks.

"I ordered them yesterday and I'm picking them up tonight," I say proudly.

"What?" he says. His tone isn't sufficiently impressed which feels surprising. Maybe he didn't hear the part where I said I ordered them YESTERDAY for TOMORROW and they will be here TODAY? Was this not a heroic level of planning?

"That doesn't make any sense. They will all be on the floor by morning, you idiot!" (He didn't really say "you idiot," but it felt very much implied.)

"What are you fucking talking about?" I yell, starting to panic. "When I was a kid we would play with helium balloons for weeks!"

"Those are the mylar ones! Not the rubber ones!" he yells back.

I run to the bathroom to google "helium balloons" and realize he's right. I have fucked up the balloons. I have ruined everything. If I'm really telling the truth here, the truth is I was sitting on a closed toilet and started lightly crying as the internet confirms a million times over that Mike is correct about the life span of rubber balloons. This wasn't the worst moment of my life by any means, but it was certainly one of the most pathetic.

I picture our child weeping in a sea of deflated balloons.

"I WILL FIX IT," I scream at Mike. "I WILL GET NEW BALLOONS IN THE MORNING."

On Yelp, some helpful soul, taking the kind of time only people who really care about other people take, had written that to get balloons at Party City you have to arrive before they open at eight because a line starts to form well before that. I head out at seven fifteen as Asher, who does not know it is his birthday, sits in a highchair, throwing yogurt on the floor.

I still don't understand LA traffic patterns, so I arrive at the store five minutes after I exit the front door of our house. I pull into the Party City parking lot to find I'm the only car here, the only person here. At first I'm annoyed—what the fuck am I going to do for forty minutes?—but after a half a second of that stupid thought, I remember the one thing every new mother learns, which is that any alone time is a gift, no matter where and when it is granted to you. I glide into the parking space closest to the entrance. It's a softly, sunny early summer morning, with that pretty California light shining upon the entire strip mall—a Souplantation, a Walgreens, a Panda Wok. I tilt my seat as far back as it will go and press play on "Hold Up." By now I have listened to this song probably three hundred times.

I'm not too perfect
To feel this worthless

The breeze flows through my car. I think about this last year. Asher's first year. My first year of being a mother. My first year of feeling like this. But what exactly is this feeling? Is this the worthlessness Beyoncé was singing about? Could Beyoncé and I possibly be experiencing any of the same things? (If so, that would make me feel one gillion times better, but since she lives on the sun and I live in the gutter that seems unlikely?) Is it just anger? Is it a cloudy weather system of just feeling generally unattractive? Thinking about it, the questions stop being questions because with nobody around I don't have to pretend that I don't know the answers. I feel frustrated and furious and horny, not to mention peeved at the fact that we as a society have never come up with a better word for horny than "horny." "Horny" feels like such a humiliating teenage-boy word, but I don't feel like a teenage boy. Or maybe—I do????

I open the windows all the way down, front and back, as I crank the music as loud as it will go. Let people look inside the brown Prius to see who is blasting Beyoncé in the parking lot of Party City. Maybe it won't be what you expect, but I didn't expect any of this. I'm done with expecting, and this is what I am now. I am a middle-aged woman, waiting for balloons.

Other cars pull up and it's almost time for Party City to open. I run to be at the front of the queue because I was VERY MUCH here first, and I can see some of these other thirsty little moms are beelining toward the door. I go inside (first) and pick up my balloons, all twenty of them. I walk out into the morning sun, open my car door, and try to stuff twenty balloons into the back seat. I make an awkward discovery, which is that it's hard to stuff twenty balloons into a Prius. They won't all fit in the back, so I have to herd a few to the front seat. Every inch of the car is occupied by either me, or balloons.

I close the car door and start driving. I think about the parties I used to go to, the men I met, the nights we made together. I wonder where they have all floated off to. Do they ever think about me? If so, what are their lasting images of me? Am I asleep? Eating a sandwich? Laughing? Naked? Handing them a drink at a bar? What do I look like in their minds? How different is it from what they would see if they were to look at me right now: a nervous wreck of a woman in a Prius filled with balloons, barely able to see the road ahead of her?

Somewhere over
the Rainbow

Having a child is a lot like having a dream.

You know how sometimes you have a dream that feels very vivid and important to you, and then when you try to tell your friend about it, they're instantly bored? Maybe they attempt to pretend to care, because ideally (or just selfishly?) most of us are trying to adhere to a social contract that dictates we stick out those moments for when it's our turn to be a needy bore.

But really, the only time someone is remotely interested in hearing about your dream is if they've had a similar one. This is why you can primarily only talk to other people with kids about your kids.

Still. Most of our own dreams are so dull that we forget them ourselves.

So many of early motherhood's tasks are endlessly repetitive, inherently forgettable drudgery. I know that I changed thousands of diapers (millions?), but, with the exception of a handful of epic blowouts, I don't remember any of them specifically.

But then there are other moments. The moments where the stars suddenly align (or maybe break apart?) and you find yourself in what feels like one of those indelible, sharply drawn surreal dreams, except for the fact that you're awake (or at least legally you're supposed to be, because you're watching a small child). Out of nowhere, some little incident unspools in the middle of the day, and suddenly, for no real reason, all your feelings come crashing down on top of you like a tidal wave; love, frustration, exhaustion, awe, sadness. Life usually gives us just one or two of these things to feel at any given time, but occasionally it seems to crumple them all up into a ball and throw them at our head just to remind us that it can.

Before I had a kid, the only way I could purposely conjure this kind of emotional flood was to visit a drive-through car wash. If you need an emotional release, there is no better cry than a car-wash cry. I like to pretend I'm in an indie film and this is our VERY special shot where I'm acting the fuck out of some melodramatic script as giant foam linguini whips soap across my windshield. Water splashes across the glass, only to then ZOOM IN as we see tears streaming down my face as well. FADE TO BLACK...

It's important to find poetry where we can.

Right when our son was in the throes of the terrible twos, Mike frequently had to travel for work, leaving Ash and me to solo adventures. Normally, things went ... fine. But during a particularly long dad business trip, we'd been having one of those mornings where there had been a plan to leave the house, but then one thing after another had spilled, and a breakfast quesadilla was served but not eaten (more specifically, he licked it, then rejected it, then it sat out on the counter for three hours before I ate it), and tantrums were had, and we both wanted to cry because this day had begun, like most days, with Asher waking up before dawn. At some point I needed to go to the bathroom. Asher had always been clingy, but once he turned two, it was as if his whole body turned to Velcro, and the idea of me going anywhere without him was a nonstarter. I started to walk to the ~~potty~~ bathroom,* but Asher grabbed my leg: "No, Mama!" I told him to play with his cars and that I would be "right back" (I really needed to go). Asher didn't give a fuck about playing with the cars. I tried gently explaining to him that sometimes (sometimes! Ha!) grown-ups want to go to the bathroom by themselves. He couldn't have been less interested in this information and Velcroed himself to my leg. I found myself lightly considering the idea of punching the wall. Sorry for what I'm about to say, but I think if you've gotten this far you can handle the truth: I really needed to shit.

I tried changing tactics. I told him he could come with me to the bathroom if he just let go of my leg. He was insulted.

---

* I have lost the ability to say the word "bathroom" anymore. Even when I'm not around children, I still say I need to go to the "potty," which is a deeply unattractive thing for a human adult to say.

Weren't we friends? Why wouldn't I want his twenty-five-pound body hanging off my thigh while I pooped? Why was I being such an asshole?

So now I really was about to cry, partially because this was all so impossible and there was no end in sight with no help for the day, and no end in sight in general. I walked with him hanging on to my leg from the bedroom to the bathroom and sat on the toilet. I pried his fingers off so I could pull my underwear down, but he promptly reattached to my bare shin.

"Asher, you've gotta give me some space." I was trying to modulate my tone so that my words sounded like a patient question, but in attempting to cover up the frustration, the frustration only became more obvious, like a bald man with a ponytail.

He clung tighter.

"Give me some space, please!"

"NO!"

Desperate, I took my phone out of my pocket. We'd already watched every episode of *Daniel Tiger's Neighborhood*, and every episode of *Splash and Bubbles*, the only two shows Asher would watch at the time. (He was extremely picky about his entertainment. I was the one mother who was trying to get him to watch more TV, and he would refuse. In fairness to him, most animated shows are terrible. We had attempted some PBS version of *Curious George*, and neither of us were into it. I could not figure out why, on a show meant for little children, screen time would frequently be taken away from George, the main star, to focus on a b-story about the Man with the Yellow Hat having a

G-rated flirtation with a teacher who works at his dinosaur museum. Who the fuck did these writers think was watching this show? Did they think either Asher or I cared about whether or not these two would BANG?*)

"Asher, do you want to watch Daniel Tiger again?"

"NO!" He let go of my leg with one hand and in one quick motion pulled half of the toilet paper off of the roll. Just as I reached to make him stop, he took the remainder of the roll and fully threw it across the bathroom, sending it streaking over the floor like a comet.

Something dark was rushing from deep within myself up to the surface, like Jaws about to breach. I felt myself getting to a place where even though I knew I would never hurt my child, the desire to do so felt terrifyingly real.

Campbell writes about the moment in the journey when the hero must cross a threshold into genuinely new and frightening territory for the first time: "Beyond them is darkness, the unknown, and danger; just as beyond the parental watch is danger to the infant . . ." In this case, I was the parental watch, and the danger to the infant felt like it was coming from—how shall we say—inside the house. It was a terrible sensation—and yet I must ask: Mothers, truly, who among us has not, at least once while raising our beloved precious perfect angels, suddenly found ourselves imagining, even for just a moment, that we are capable of doing unimaginable things? We don't talk

---

* I actually did care a little bit. Also, isn't the Man with the Yellow Hat gay?

about this enough. We just live with the secret feeling of being guilty little monsters. But I believe pushing through those moments, forcing ourselves to get our shit together, is one of motherhood's most heroic acts. It can be so fucking HARD. And yet we don't even feel like we can talk about it.

Anyway. I'm not sure why or how it came to me. I think I just knew we were in dire enough straits that we didn't need to be entertained, we needed to be transported. I tried to recall what had truly transported me when I was a child.

At this particular moment, I hadn't watched *The Wizard of Oz* in decades. But somehow Dorothy appeared to me when I needed her most. I typed "Somewhere over the Rainbow" into YouTube with one hand, as Asher pulled at the other. I prayed to mom-on-the-toilet Jesus that the link wouldn't be behind ten ads. But with one tap, as if I had clicked my heels, there was Judy Garland.

And wouldn't you know it, the minute she started singing, Asher was transfixed. He slid to the floor and settled. I put my phone on the bathroom floor, and we both watched the song begin to unfurl, those first famous notes slowly stretching the word "somewhere" into a journey all its own.

Somewhere over the rainbow
Way up high

And as Asher watched, making not a peep, I got hit by that tidal wave of car-wash feeling, this confluence of past and present, of five-year-old me intertwined with present-day me, and

I couldn't stop thinking about how I couldn't possibly know, as a five-year-old girl in 1980 watching *The Wizard of Oz* on my parents' TV, that one day I would be a ragged, chronically depressed forty-two-year-old weirdo, sitting on a toilet; that at my feet in this same tableau would sit my beautiful little boy in his diaper and T-shirt, staring at a device that wouldn't be invented for another twenty-seven years; and that the sweet Dorothy I was watching with nothing but wonder would later be understood by me to be Judy Garland, who had died of drugs and heartbreak and depression; and that I would summon her, like my own Glinda the Good Witch, to please get me out of here. Judy would appear and elevate this utterly mundane scene, a tired mother and her annoyed toddler son, into something just a bit more magical. Or maybe she was really just helping reveal it for what it already was: a minute of shared human wistfulness for everything to be different. All three of us, Asher and Dorothy and me, dreaming of being somewhere else, but, each in our own way, momentarily present for the beauty of the longing.

At the end of the movie, Dorothy, of course, wakes up. The whole adventure was a dream. Her family is gathered around, but when she tries to tell them about her dream—the very story we just spent two hours watching, riveted, a movie about one of the greatest journeys of all time that has enthralled generations—not one of them cares! They smile and humor her, but seriously, when you rewatch, they don't even want to hear a thing about it! Which is surprising because usually the one thing that perks you up about someone else's dream is if they say you were in it! But the whole family was in her dream and not one of them gives a single fuck! She tries to tell them details, but they won't even bother giving her a perfunctory listen. "Some of it wasn't very nice," she says, "but most of it was beautiful." "There, there," she's told, as the men who populated the dream chuckle at the insanity of this young girl they all seem to be pretending to care about.

I think about Dorothy going through life with the Oz dream always on her mind, her worldview and aspirations forever impacted by this vivid vision, but having no one with whom she can share it. The dream was real to her, and the way it changed her was real, but everyone around her thinks she's just babbling nonsense. She went on an epic journey, but is then told she didn't. Will she write it down? Or will the denial by those around her of what she's been through make her doubt that anyone else would care?

I don't remember changing thousands of diapers; I don't know what I will remember in the future; but I know I will always remember the two of us listening to Judy sing in my bathroom. I remember yearning for another adult to have witnessed this moment with me, to have another person who felt what it felt like: big, important, profound.

Being a parent is a lot like having a dream. Some of it isn't very nice. Most of it, even when it's ugly, is beautiful.

Your Husband Will Remarry Five Minutes After You Die

The concept of dying is already depressing enough. The last thing I want to think about is the possibility of someone hurting my feelings after I'm dead. Actually, not having my feelings hurt seems like one of the few advantages of no longer being alive. But as a wife, I can't help but notice that husbands tend to get remarried approximately five minutes after their wife's heart stops. I know I'm a sensitive little orchid, but I still can't help but feel a certain anticipatory anxiety that should I ever find myself in this scenario (dead), and if Mike were to re-marry so quickly, some jealousy nerve deep in my soul, which normally would be in dormant death mode, would reflexively activate, the way a chicken's body supposedly can keep on running after its head has been cut off.

It's not that I don't want him to remarry—I do. (But if he didn't, I'd be fine? I just want him to be happy. Happy-ish?) I'm more concerned with how extraordinarily quickly this spousal replacement seems to happen, and the degree of enthusiasm that we, the dead and/or dying wives, are supposed to muster for this common turn of events, even while we're alive. There exists this romanticized notion that we're supposed to give our husbands not just permission but even encouragement to find someone new, sometimes before we're even diagnosed as terminal (maybe even on days where it seems like we might be taking a turn for the better?). That's because we're angels and we're giving and what's most important to us is that our husbands *go on*. Still, even the most angelic among us probably wishes that if and when the time comes, the convo might go something like this:

Dying Wife: I'm dying.
Husband: I'm distraught beyond words.
Dying Wife: I want you to know that after I pass, I want you to find love again—
Husband: Stop. I will never love anyone as much as you. You're the love of my life, and I . . . [unintelligible weeping.]

. . . and scene.

Unfortunately, I suspect the conversation more often goes like this:

Dying Wife: I'm—
Husband: I've met someone.
Dying Wife: What?

Husband: Doctor, I think we should pull the plug. I know she wouldn't want to live like this.

Dying Wife: The surgeon is saying I have a really good chance at making a full recovery—

Husband: She's hallucinating, she must be in pain, pull the plug, Doctor! I don't have time to argue about this, I'm meeting my girlfriend in five minutes.

Doctor: Sir, she's not plugged into anything.

When I was little, my dad told me there wasn't enough love to go around in the world and so we must be happy when anyone finds it. After decades of observation I would say in general I AGREE. All I want in this life is for no one to be lonely. I'm truly not judging any individuals for their choices after the loss of a spouse (unless they killed them, in which case 'FESS UP). And I admit that I'm probably projecting my own issues here; I hold on to every emotion with the desperate tenacity of those novelty koalas we used to clip onto our pencils in the '70s. I recognize that most humans are able to get over people and events and move on; that's part of what makes the human spirit "indomitable" or whatever they call it in movie trailers.

And yet, perhaps we could just acknowledge for a quick min the ways in which his future happiness without you can be a smidge crushing to ponder. Shall we give ourselves permission to just let it all out for the next few minutes without guilt, and then we'll go back to being our very best (dead one day) selves? LET'S DO IT.

Part of the reason the collective female mind boggles at

seeing men move on so quickly is that women generally don't do this. Women tend to outlive their husbands, and when they do, their reaction is not to immediately remarry but to finally lean into their own lives. There's the trope that men are dogs and women are cats. That you can leave a cat alone and as long as you leave water and a bag of kibble that they can tip over, they'll be fine. If you leave a dog alone, even with food and water and a gym membership and thirty years' worth of frozen meals and written instructions for finding a local social group to join, they'll shit the bed for a while and then starve to death. Women grieve and are sad, but then they gradually forge forward and start exploring all the interests they set aside for decades when they were taking care of their husband and kids. They remember that once, long ago, before they got married and had babies, they were interested in reading books about capybaras, and now they get up and go to the library and get that capybara book and make themselves a smoothie and sit in their house and read that book. They take painting classes or learn a language or even just stay in their house in bed and eat a stack of pancakes like no one's watching. After my grandfather died, my incredibly sparky, gorgeous grandma joined the local senior center, making necklaces and painting watercolor palm trees and socializing. She lived in her own house until she was ninety-seven and had a full head of hair and loved the New York Mets and the Home Shopping Network. In bewildered tones, she'd tell me about the stream of old dudes who were trying to be her boyfriend. "I don't want nothin' with them," she'd say, and then proudly present me with the most recent string of beads she'd made.

My future dead feelings are further injured when I think about how, for so many of us, marriage was a less-than-fave topic among our future surviving spouses. When it came to proposing, my husband (and I say this with all love, etc., etc.) took his time? It would be tough to hear that if/when he meets his next wife, he'll be trying to lock it down in the same amount of time it took for us to negotiate a space for me to leave a ponytail holder on the outermost edge of the sink. The fact that some of this might be driven less by romance than by the urgent need for someone to now be his assistant/lover/chef might lessen the pang of it all, but not by much, I don't think, especially given the fact that, statistically speaking in these situations, she will probably be, at most, twenty-fawn years old.

I just want to be missed. Deeply and profoundly missed for an uninterrupted amount of time, hungering for my presence with no cheat days. It just doesn't seem to me you can really *focus* on *properly* missing someone if you're busy having sex with your twenty-six-year-old second wife, which is actually why I think older men need twenty-six-year-old second wives so badly—not just for the sex they get to have, but for the thoughts they get to not have.

If he were alone, there wouldn't be anything to distract him from feeling regret, love, sadness; there would be time for the one person on Earth who loved me the most—and knew me intimately and watched me pee with the door open for years—to do nothing but remember me, and in doing so keep me just a bit more alive. And, I mean, of course, yes, I KNOW it's possible for men to do this while dating or married to someone else. It's just that I suspect that many of them don't, or won't, and that's because my experience of men is that they love to compartmentalize, and it's easier to compartmentalize your recently dead wife when you're helping your twenty-three-year-old girlfriend make her TikToks? (I know a second ago I referred to this woman as twenty-six, but I'm pretty sure the longer I'm dead the younger she gets.)

The compartmentalizing is what hurts the worst. Being put in a coffin and stuffed into the soil is already not what you'd call a DREAM SCENARIO; the one little hopeful bit is that some people will keep your memory going aboveground. And yet the window of time between a man becoming a widower and the uploading of his picture on Hinge is so often paper-thin. I'll admit, most of my resentment stems from jealousy; as someone who has never been able to compartmentalize even one fucking aspect of my life, I can tell you, I don't recommend it. Imagine carrying around literally everything you own in your arms twenty-four hours a day, including forks and knives and all your emotions and USB cords, and never being able to put one thing down. This so often seems to be the opposite of what a man does, which is to have a feeling, go to the Container Store, find an airtight plastic bin that fits the feeling exactly, put the feeling into the bin, tell the bin he wants to take it on a romantic boat ride, row the boat to the middle of the ocean, and push the bin over the side, later telling the cops through fake tears that there was a storm and he couldn't do anything to save it. Wait, what were we talking about again? Oh, right, bins.

I recognize that neither of the mental health models I'm describing is ideal, and that the most reasonable way to deal with your life is probably somewhere in between what men do (bins, boats) and what I do (running in infinite circles with all my emotions in my arms). (And look, I realize I'm speaking in very broad terms here but I'M ALMOST DONE.)

By now maybe you're asking yourself, *How long is he supposed to wait, after all? What amount of time would feel like enough?* Or maybe you're not asking—maybe I'm just asking myself. Aghhh, I don't know. A month definitely feels too short. A year maybe feels too long? Although maybe it's perfect? The more I try to think about what would be respectful both to his needs and mine, the more I feel self-conscious about the degree to which I'm coming off as too selfish. I'll be gone, what does it matter, why am I clinging? Maybe I should just stop. Maybe I should just let this go.

But then my future ghost rattles her chains and howls, and I finish typing this anyway.

Talismans

It has become a thing, a rite of passage almost like giving birth itself, that once you become a mom you have to get some piece of jewelry emblazoned with your kid's initials, or their name, or their birth date or star chart. There are also now about two million bracelets, necklaces, signet rings, and little gold discs you can buy engraved with MAMA or MOM or MOTHER. I don't know when this happened. Has it always been this way? I don't remember my mother having anything like this when I was growing up, or anyone else's mother, for that matter. But the minute I gave birth to my kid and started going to baby gyms and kid parties, I began to notice all the other moms clanking about with little bits of metal around their necks and wrists stamped OLIVER and MARLO and ZEUS. *What is this stuff?* I asked myself. *Am I a bad mom if I don't have it? Do I not love my kid if I don't have his name dangling somewhere off my actual person? And, regardless of the answers to these questions—do I want it?*

I mean, part of me did want it. I like jewelry and I'm all too ready to T-shirt-cannon some cash at a silly trinket. But at the same time, a part of me also felt some deep, visceral resistance to this trend; I couldn't quite put my finger on why, but my reaction was a blend of resentment, embarrassment, and anxiety. I guess the shorthand for this stew would be to say I found this stuff somehow . . . triggering.

Trigger 1: I have always been a fool for a talisman. Part of me of course knows better than to pretend an object will give me magical powers; yet that part of me is no match for the part of me that does not.* If there is some kind of charm bracelet that I can pretend keeps my child safe, of course I will order it (I mean, maybe not pay for it to be sent overnight, but two-day delivery, if that's an option). Still, it's hard not to feel like the charm industrial complex is monetizing all our darkest anxieties. No one likes to be taken advantage of by a complex.

One million years ago, I worked at *Saturday Night Live*, and about six weeks into the job I realized I was terrible at it. On Tuesday nights, which were the writing nights, I would feel an endless creeping nausea, and during the entire Wednesday table read (a torturous four-to-five-hour session that required an intermission), I would wish for nothing more than the ability to spontaneously evaporate, a professional humiliation-driven version of the Rapture, as line after line of the sketches I'd written would sink like a stone. After a couple of months of, com-

---

* This is the same part of me that denies the reality that liquids can have any calories even while Weight Watchers makes it abundantly clear that four measly ounces of white wine is FIVE FUCKING POINTS.

edically speaking, fully eating shit every week, the stress of constantly bombing in front of all my coworkers (plus my boss, who you may have heard of? Lorne Michaels? Jewish Canadian fellow) was leading to something that felt a lot like a nervous breakdown. I was terrified of turning in sketches, knowing that they would fail.

Because I never got any of my material on the show, during rehearsal days—Thursdays and Fridays—I would find myself stuck at my desk for hours with nothing to do, and I would just sit in an anxious little ball staring at the internet until one day I decided maybe what I needed to do was to start searching out jewelry featuring empowering words and mantras, because obviously this was a way better use of my time than trying to come up with better sketch ideas. I found two things of interest: a little rectangle pendant made by a high-end boutique stamped with the word FEARLESSNESS on both sides (English on the front, Sanskrit on the back); and then, at a lower price point, I found an Etsy artisan who made "spinner rings," a kind of lo-fi wearable precursor to a fidget spinner, engraved with motivational phrases. Imagine my delight when I saw the one emblazoned with THIS TOO SHALL PASS. I imagined bombing at the Tuesday table read while spinning the spinner ring, waiting for my sketch to shall-pass. I fully believed that the dreaded three minutes during which my sketch was read aloud would be much more endurable if I was quietly meditating by spinning my witchy little power ring.

Torn over whether to buy FEARLESSNESS or THIS TOO SHALL PASS, I decided I couldn't function without either of these incredible pieces and treated myself to both. You're probably wondering if I now realize how self-indulgent this all sounds, and the answer is a resounding yes. And if you're hoping I was in some way karmically punished for spending money in such a frivolous manner, don't worry: both the ring and the necklace were the fails I deserved. As soon as I opened the box in which the spinner ring arrived, I realized it didn't look quite the way it had on the website. It was much larger and chunkier than I had pictured and less delicately made. Still, I figured the form didn't matter as much as the function, which was to make me feel magically better, so even though the ring, once on, made me look like I had one steampunk-style robotic finger, I still committed to wearing it. On Wednesday morning I put it on and walked into the conference room filled with mostly male comedy writers and immediately felt like I was some kind of Coachellan hippie in huge feather earrings. When it was my sketch's turn to be read and it (inevitably) tanked again, I fiddled with my ring and realized now I was the writer who not only consistently bombed but in addition constantly fiddled with my accessories like a mental patient. I took it off that night and never put it on again.

Meanwhile, the FEARLESSNESS necklace had also arrived. It was actually quite pretty. It was dainty but not so dainty that you couldn't make out the word "FEARLESSNESS," which made me happy because I wanted everyone to see how FEARLESSNESS I was. I wore that necklace every day for a few weeks until I ran into another woman I knew wearing the same exact one. I had always been struck by her frantic, terrified energy, which the necklace actually seemed to amplify rather than decrease. Then a few weeks later I saw yet *another* woman I knew wearing the FEARLESSNESS necklace. She was a permanently agitated person, constantly radiating the energy of a yappy Yorkie tied to a pole outside a shop. I realized that the necklace was less a talisman than an obvious tell. It's like how at an office the person with the KEEP CALM AND CARRY ON poster prominently displayed on their wall is almost always the person screaming most loudly into their phone.

Trigger 2: I have always been suspicious of groups, primarily because I was allowed into so few of them growing up. The only thing that made me feel worse than groups were the passive-aggressive/aggressive ways people in groups signaled their groupings. See: pairs of mean girls holding hands.* People chanting "USA" at sporting events. Having always felt like an outsider, it's hard for me to shed the outsider's perspective; I've always carried a kind of survivors' guilt about the potential for a demonstration of group identity to accidentally make someone else feel excluded. As someone who struggled with infertility, I still vividly remember the sinking feeling of not being able to turn anywhere without seeing diaper ads and strollers and pregnant bellies, and with those experiences in mind, I

---

* I have girlfriends I love, whom I would marry, but I have never held hands with them. I love platonic heterosexual men holding hands, gay women holding hands, gay men holding hands, children holding hands, and otters holding hands, but straight high school girls platonically holding hands is and always will be a red flag to me.

feel a twinge at the idea of wearing a mini billboard about my momhood.

Long before I even wanted kids, right around when I turned thirty, I suddenly noticed that the holiday cards I was receiving were all turning into family photographs of my now-new-parent friends. Beginning the week after Thanksgiving, the cards would start arriving, glossy postcards with a picture of mom and dad and baby and, somehow always, dog. People I didn't know had a dog would suddenly have a dog. There they all are, sitting on their stoop in the suburbs, baby in the middle, dog (how long have they had this dog?), and across the picture in swooping holiday script it says HAPPY HOLIDAYS FROM JOHN, JESSICA, THATCHER, AND MR. PIBS. Mr. Pibs is in a Santa hat. A few years later, another child has been added to the card, which now reads HAPPY HOLIDAYS FROM JOHN, JESSICA, THATCHER, AVA, AND POCKETS. (Apparently, Mr. Pibs passed.)

To be clear, I love all the people who send these cards, and I also love their kids, and frankly I'm jealous they have the time for pets. And I KNOW it is not the intention of my dear friends sending these cards to turn opening my mail into a lightly shattering sensation of feeling less-than. And yet, as my single, childless, microwave-less self began heating up a frozen Amy's burrito in a pan to eat alone while watching Anderson Cooper, that was how I felt.

The question of what to do with these photo missives was a whole other rain cloud. Regular Hallmark cards could be thrown almost instantaneously into the garbage, but chucking photos of babies into the recycling felt at best disrespectful and at worst somehow like casting a curse? And yet the alternative ideas, such as displaying them up on my fridge, seemed empirically worse. What's creepier than displaying photos of other people's kids in your home? Honestly, the only other idea I can come up with is keeping photos of my friends' kids stashed in a drawer, so garbage it is. Why do we keep doing this? Why do my friends want me to throw pictures of their children in the trash? Now that I have my own kid, I can confirm I still have no urge to deal with printing and sending an annual picture of our family to anyone else. (I do want to get a dog and dress it up, but I would do this on any day of the week, not just holidays.) Now that I have a kid, even with just the one, I am so constantly underwater that if I wanted to arrange for this photo to be taken, I don't know how I would find the time, and even if I did find the time it would end up being a picture of me with a mustache because there is no way I have the time to get the card done and have my mustache waxed.*

Nevertheless. In spite of all of this, I still found myself down the personalized baby jewelry rabbit hole. Late into the night, in line at the bank, waiting at a grocery store, sitting in my bedroom, I became obsessed with the available options, of which there were a dillion. I spent hours and hours, time in which

---

* The mustache is always last on my list. Only by getting everything else done that I possibly have to do in my life do I allow myself the indulgence of going to get the hair ripped off of my face. I suppose I could get it lasered off permanently, but I'm worried that if my 'stache never grew back I would lose the urgency of getting anything else done?

I could have been writing, or exercising, or waxing my mustache, searching for this piece, wanting it to be perfect. Why, really, was I doing this? Was this really going to be my version of the mythical protective talisman that Joseph Campbell writes about?

Or maybe there was something else going on?

I think something else was going on.

The something else was that the other thing I could have been doing while searching for jewelry to engrave with my child's name was actually playing with my own child.

And yet at this moment in time, my son was just a little over two and we were in the midst of the most animal-like fights over eating, sleeping, and in general, how to be a person. He wanted to be more like a raccoon, and I wanted him to be more like a human; and in trying to cajole and beg him to do that, I turned into a raccoon myself, a large female one who didn't sleep or eat enough and was cranky all the time because of it. So essentially, in trying to teach him how to be more like me, I became him.

How satisfying that I could be searching for something that would give me the appearance of being a loving and connected mother, when in fact the search itself was a reason to hide in my room and get on the internet to look for, let's be honest, a gift for my damn self. I suddenly understood that for all of these mothers toting around this baby-name bling, it was less a tribal marking or a talisman than it was just one tangible little trophy for surviving this experience. One little reward for walking around like a ghost of yourself most of the time. And yeah, of course there are the rewards of your child saying "I love you" for the first time or giving you a hug or watching them take their first steps or any of the other tearjerkers they put in diaper ads, but as my wise friend Kelly once said to me: "Sometimes you just need something to come in the mail."

I ended up getting a delicate hexagonal gold plate with Asher's first and middle name engraved in black enamel, all caps, custom-made by a local jeweler. It's been two years since I bought it, and I still love it and wear it all the time. This year, he turned four and I turned forty-four. A few weeks before my birthday, I wandered into my favorite neighborhood store and peeked into the jewelry case, where I saw a sweet little ID bracelet, something I've wanted since I was twelve. All the cool girls in my junior high school (the ones who held hands) had them. This one was subtle and relatively inexpensive, and after sleeping on it for a weekend, I decided I would buy it, partially justifying the purchase by thinking this could be another piece with Asher's name—or maybe this one would be his birth date. Or perhaps a combo of our first initials, A & J.

But then I had an absolutely crazy idea: What if I just engraved it with my own name? Jessi. That's it. Just my name. Nothing about my kid or my family or the latitude or longitude of his birthplace. At first this felt genuinely wild, indulgent, selfish. But then I thought, how crazy is it that wanting the name on my ID bracelet to be the name that identifies me feels like some kind of crime, as if I had left Asher alone in the living room watching *Daniel Tiger* while I went to snort meth in my car.

I bought the bracelet and had it engraved in script with my name, a capital "J" and lowercase "essi." The ID bar of the bracelet is extremely thin, a few centimeters, so the letters themselves are minuscule; my entire name is about the size of a black ant. It's hard to see, but I know it's there, and I find it to be more of a comfort than I expected. I'll forget about it until a moment happens like the one that occurred the other afternoon, when one of Asher's little friends was here for a playdate. Teddy, a sweet boy I adore who's been one of Asher's best buddies for years, plays here all the time. On the hunt for a juice box, he came running across the house, calling for me by saying: "Asher's mom! Asher's mom! Can I please have a juice box, Asher's mom?"

Teddy was confident this was my name. The only question in his mind was whether Asher's mom would grant him the juice box. I was hiding in my bedroom like I always did during the second half of long playdates. I was trying to write, and I couldn't figure out what I wanted to say or how to say it, but Teddy needed help. So I got up and went to the pantry and became Asher's Mom. And I have to admit, I could see in Teddy's eyes how impressed he was by Asher's Mom, this woman who could open the pantry, reach the high shelf, pull down a juice box, and then stab the foil hole open with the sharp plastic straw like it was no big deal. He said thank you (Teddy's always polite, God bless this kid), and then I went back to my room to be Jessi again, the forty-four-year-old woman wondering if she still has a story to tell.

Bread and Cheese

A sher is five and a half and won't eat anything but bread and cheese.

It's enraging. Enraaaging. (That said, truthfully, I am forty-five and I too want to eat only bread and cheese, and on many days I do, because now I'm in charge of taking care of myself, which means often I don't.) But still. This doesn't seem like a great diet for a growing child, or really, anyone.

I'll back up. Maybe "nothing but bread and cheese" is an exaggeration. There's a little more. This is the full list of what he currently, as of this moment, eats:

- Bread
- Rice
- Pasta (plain or mac and cheese. Which is basically plain pasta, but with cheese.)
- Quinoa
- Cheese (Babybel cheese, string cheese, pieces of Tillamook mild cheddar.)

- Pizza (although it better be plain and it better be NY style and if there is even one shred of basil the size of a pencil point on there, you're gonna hear about it. We count pizza as a separate food from bread and cheese because it does involve tomato sauce. That said, tomato sauce isn't on the list because it is only ever eaten in the form of pizza, never on pasta.)
- Scrambled eggs
- Chicken noodle soup from Gelson's
- Peanut butter and jelly sandwiches
- Bananas
- Graham crackers
- Goldfish*
- Apples
- Applesauce
- Chips
- Cake
- Cookies
- Chicken fingers (a little bit, sometimes)
- Cereal

That's it. That's all the foods he eats. Looking at the list, I realize this may seem like a lot of foods. But you have to understand—right now—this is truly it. This is IT. Every day. I have to pretend, for my own sanity, that the applesauce and apples I'm feeding him multiple times a day are somehow dif-

---

* Probably shouldn't be on the list because obviously Goldfish are not a food.

ferent nutrients even though they really aren't, or I will drive my car into the Pacific Ocean from frustration.

Of all the childhood behaviors that trigger me—whining, procrastinating, tantrum-ing—Asher's refusal to eat is the one that makes me most want to tantrum myself. It feels like the ultimate betrayal: I grew you in my body, I birthed you, I gave you life, how dare you now refuse to do this most basic of staying-alive activities? If you do not eat, you will die, but also, if you keep not eating, I might strangle you? There's really no winning.

It's not like I don't relate to it. I was an extremely picky eater as a child—no vegetables, no unknown sauces, nothing with weird textures. I only began to change when I finally found friends around fourth grade, and I felt sufficient shame in the experience of not being able to eat what they were eating that I gradually expanded my palate. Still, I've never forgotten how uncomfortable it was to be the weird, difficult one, and to this day when I eat sushi I still feel like I'm a very sophisticated, worldly global citizen—basically like I'm Cate Blanchett. Not that the irrational selectiveness has left me entirely. I still struggle with a certain kind of white food, primarily any sort of curdled dairy: sour cream, cream cheese, yogurt, cottage cheese, and for fuck's sake, do not even try to come near me with mayonnaise. But for the most part, I've grown out of it. I have a friend, however, who did not—at age forty-three, he continues to eat the same children's menu type diet he ate when he was five, existing to this day on pizza, hot dogs, and little else.

This is apparently a real disorder known as adult picky eater syndrome. Aside from how this may affect his physical health, it causes him a real amount of emotional suffering.

I do not want Asher to have adult picky eater syndrome.

We started off following all the instructions, introducing a little mushed baby food when he was around five months old. Just to be extra precious about it, we had our own baby food maker, in which we pureed squash and peas at home. Asher would poke at this mush a bit and seemed to be eating as normally as the next baby, which is to say, a large part of every meal ended up on the walls and the floor. Out of every batch of lovingly made mush, maybe a thimbleful ended up in his body. However, this seemed par for the course, and given that everything he was being offered to eat looked very much like barf, he was interested enough.

As Asher got a little older, we started buying "pouches." I do not think these existed when I was a kid, which makes me question how anyone survived to adulthood, considering how essential they are to children now. If you're not familiar with these pouches,* they are basically little squeezie plastic things

---

* It occurred to me at one point, as I was discovering these pouches, that an adult interested in carving off ten pounds could maybe reliably do so in a not-completely-unhealthy way if they were to perhaps just eat pouches for a month? I wondered if this had occurred to anyone else and went to google it and, wouldn't you know it, an article immediately popped up titled "Adults: Stop Eating Food Out of Pouches."

filled with purees of fruits and vegetables (and, shudder, some-times "turkey"? Even though they're not kept in the refriger-ated food section of the supermarket? SHUDDER). They have little plastic caps, and you basically unscrew the cap and tooth-paste the contents into your kid's mouth and pray that feed-ing them twelve of these a day counts as sustenance? There are many brands, and within each brand, different flavors are color-coded. Right off the bat, Asher's favorite flavors involved bananas—as you can see, still on the list to this day—and there were two colors of banana pouch, a pure yellow for just banana, and then a purple one that was banana and spinach. For a while we could feed him both the purple and the yellow pouches. But one day, we were at the park and when it came time for a snack I reached for the purple pouch and Asher said, "No, yelo." For a few weeks after I could still blurp a purple pouch into his mouth, especially if he was strapped into his stroller, but pretty soon he started turning his head away from purple altogether. Which means our already admittedly shabby way of getting any kind of vegetable or vegetable-adjacent substance into him—half of a store-bought mush pack—was now failing. Still, I told myself, at least he was eating . . . pouch fruit?

We enrolled Asher in preschool. Of all the items I had to buy in the emotional swirl of prepping for the momentous first day, the lunch box gave me the most anxiety. I am almost certain that when I was a child my lunch box was divided into just two sections, one for your solids and one for your thermos-ed liq-uid. But today, there are dozens of versions of bento boxes with fifty different compartments for putting—what?—every food group? Our family was working with only three: bread, cheese, and water. What do they think is going in here?

And yet, during the first week of school, when I arrived for pickup (which was at the end of lunchtime), I noticed that all the other kids also had these same kinds of bento boxes and their parents had in fact FILLED ALL THE FUCKING COMPARTMENTS WITH DIFFERENT HEALTHY FOODS. Half of these kids—TWO-YEAR-OLDS—were consuming RAW BROCCOLI. A boy on Asher's right was eating a piece of FUCKING SEAWEED. One kid had the nerve to pop a cherry tomato straight into his mouth like it was nothing. Meanwhile, Asher was finishing eating one of the bread slices from his PB&J, and the only other food in his bento box was a bag of chips. I clipped his lunch box shut, put it in his Curious George backpack, took Asher's hand, and fled.

I continued to see this pattern over the next few months. Other kids were advancing in the breadth of their palates, while we remained mired in the land of bread and cheese. One night we had one of Asher's little school buddies and her family over for a late-afternoon playdate. Too exhausted to make dinner on a Sunday night, I suggested takeout: "How about sushi for us and pizza for the kids?" "Well," her dad said, "she's actually cool with sushi too." "Ah," I said. An hour later, as I watched this three-year-old happily munch down a yellowtail scallion roll, I had to go to the bathroom, lock the door, and take five deep breaths.

———

I scoured the internet for toddler recipes. There are now a million popular Instagram accounts created by mothers sharing daily lunch recipes that use bread and cheese and/or fun, funky shapes to Trojan Horse actual nutrients into their kids' meals. They're littered with pictures of star-shaped kiwis, dinosaur-shaped sandwiches, and rocket ship–shaped zucchini fritters. All of these accounts made me want to get into a dry tub and curl into the fetal position. I'm a lousy cook—just making something healthy and edible feels like enough of a challenge. The idea that it also has to be Insta-ready seems like a snooch much.

After perusing dozens of recipes, I decide I'm going to make him an asparagus risotto. I don't remember where the recipe came from, but I choose it because it seems easy enough to make and doesn't have to end up in a specific shape. Its shape is gloop. It combines some of Asher's favorite flavors (grain and cheese), but the other key component (asparagus) basically makes it a superfood, and me a saint. I print the recipe out. Truly, there were probably about four steps to this whole thing, but for me this was a very big deal. I put the already wrinkled recipe print-out on a wooden book stand like I am goddamn Julia Child. The first thing I do is chop the asparagus into molecule-sized pieces, so small you would need the Hadron Collider to find these green bits in the risotto.

While our nanny, Lucy, plays with Asher in the living room, I stir and steam away. I pour myself a little glass of wine because aren't you always supposed to have just one little glass of wine while you're cooking? It is late afternoon, shafts of golden sunlight pour into the kitchen, and I begin to feel a new persona coming on: me as wholesome nurturer, a Barefoot Contessa type, an earth queen reigning over my warm hearth.

After thirty minutes of agonizing attention to every detail of this four-step recipe, I take a bite of my creation. It tastes like cheese rice. Which I suppose means it's a successful enough risotto? There is not a trace of asparagus flavor. Which I suppose means it's a successful kid entrée?

Finally, it's finished cooking, and I prepare to serve it, ready to receive my Michelin Star. Lucy puts Asher in his booster seat as I lovingly spoon the meal onto Asher's most special plastic dish (it has a picture of the Eiffel Tower on it). I put the plate onto Asher's tray and also give him his finest plastic spoon (it has a picture of a bear on it). This is a classy operation, babyyyyyy!!!! Move over, French Laundry, because We. Are. Ser. Ving. Class.

Asher looks down at the risotto and says he doesn't want it. I'm a little surprised, but that's okay.

"It's so yummy!" I say, like a thirsty little bitch.

"Don't want."

"Let's just try it."

"No."

"C'mon, one bite."

"No."

I'm a bit puzzled at his reaction because this meal is his favorite food colors, white and tan. But that's okay. Okay okay

okay, we can do this. I'm not mad I'm not mad I'm not mad, even though—I'm definitely getting mad? Having finished my glass of wine, I crack open a beer. I place an irresistibly delicate little amount of the risotto on the spoon. In the '80s, that "posh" cat food brand Fancy Feast ran a series of ads where a butler (ha) would fork their wet kibble into a close-up glamour shot, with some kind of crystal decanter in the background to convince everyone at home this was the most delicious shit in the world.

This moment was kind of like that.

But Asher still won't open his mouth.

I gently put the spoon to his lips.

He turns his head away.

Now I am mad.

I am mad, and he is hungry. We are in that familiar spiral: In order to get him to try something new, I can't give him other choices, no matter how *Reservoir Dogs* our standoff is getting. However, a picky child who is even slightly hungry can be a fucking nightmare. Their behavior immediately becomes terrible, and the only way you can get them to stop being terrible is to feed them. But their fear of new food is greater than their need to eat. You can't buckle and let them win or the entire power structure comes tumbling down and then it'll be anarchy. You have to overpower their will with the strength of yours, which is a weird feeling because before I had a child I didn't have a ton of practice with trying to OVERPOWER ANYONE'S WILL. It's uncomfortable, trying to crush another person's desires. But apparently little children are fine with it because they know the need to make them stop screaming will be greater than the need to make them eat good food, and so they never give up. So now you are back in the cycle of feeding them garbage and your Barefoot Contessa fantasy is shattered.

I yell at Asher to eat the risotto. He screams back that he will not. I look at Lucy, who has diplomatically, heroically even, moved into another room. I tell her I need to take a walk and storm out the door.

At the time of this culinary showdown, we lived on a pretty, winding street, and it was a gorgeous spring day, the sun just settling into golden hour; the kind of rare LA afternoon where you can wear whatever you want—remove a layer and feel perfectly brisk, add a layer and feel cozy. Surrounded by this beautiful tableau, I stomped along, bubbling with rage. I had yelled at my child. And for this, I was terrible. He wouldn't eat, and for this, he was terrible. We were both terrible. Everything was terrible.

As I galumphed around a bend, I saw a woman, about eighty feet away, walking her dog in my direction. Even from that distance, she caught my eye. She was wearing black leggings and clogs, and a white tank top under an open plaid flannel shirt. She had long blonde hair. There was something about the ease and slowness of her gait, letting her dog lead and stop to sniff whatever, and then go again. Between her walk, her legs in the leggings, and her casually messy hair glinting gold in the sun, she was clearly beautiful. I hated her. I hated that she was out for a leisurely walk with her dog, that she wasn't thirty pounds overweight, I hated that she hadn't just yelled at a toddler for not consuming the mediocre meal she'd made for him—I hated everything about her . . . until the moment I got close enough to see that she was, in fact, someone I knew who I quite liked. She was Hannah, an old friend's girlfriend who I ran into a few times a year, and she was always lovely—funny, smart, warm, friendly. An actual gem of a gal.

While I was deciding whether I could handle saying hello, Hannah recognized me and walked over. "Hi!" she said, giving me a big smile. "How are you?" I smiled and tried to be light and funny, and not talk about what had just happened, but twenty seconds into the conversation I found myself babbling the word "risotto," and trying to be humorous about my child who wouldn't eat, when in fact I was disturbed down to my core. Hannah, being the champ that she is, laughed about it too, but I felt like she could see right through me, even though absolutely nothing in her sweet demeanor betrayed this. It was more that as I described the problem, I saw right through myself, and what I saw was someone who just could not take a small child's refusals lightly. It all weighed so heavy; I could never find my way to the sitcom-mother version of exasperation that so many movies and TV shows had taught me I was supposed to accept—that kind of soft, middle-of-the-road, passing miff that exists just long enough to get laughs and then evaporates as quickly as it appeared. I can't think of a time I've seen a "good" mom really and truly lose her temper at a young child on TV. We see plenty of moms snapping at surly teens, and we're all fine with it, because who doesn't want to see a surly teen put in their place? But when it comes to representation of mothers losing their patience with little kids—like really and truly losing it in an unappealing way such as, oh, I don't know, hypothetically speaking, yelling and then storming out of the room—wouldja believe there seems to be less of an appetite to see this on-screen? And yet—I don't know a mom who hasn't done this at least once?

After a few minutes we said goodbye, and I watched her go, clogs clip-clopping, high, young, childless tush swaying gently along. (This was when I was still in my elastic-waisted-ankle-length-Splendid-skirt period.) She didn't seem to be yelling at her dog for not eating, or for sniffing the grass, or for anything. In fact, they seemed to get along great. I wanted so badly to be her. Her, or the dog. Either would have been fine.

Back at the house, Mike was already getting Asher, who'd ended up getting a banana pouch for dinner, ready for his bath. I went to the cupboard and grabbed a newly opened bag of blue chips. I started mindlessly chomping, neither hungry nor full, just plowing my way through the bag, and continuing along even as I got to the bottom, the size of the chips getting smaller and smaller until I had to use a spoon to keep going. When I was done with the chips, I tucked into the pot of leftover risotto still sitting on the stove.

Change of Hands

Before our son was born, Mike was insistent we would need a night nurse, but I wasn't sure. I thought of my parents, who took care of us three kids with basically no extra help ever. The idea of hiring someone to do the work of staying up with the baby we created triggered all my deeply ingrained class issues; a little voice inside of me kept screaming, WHO DO YOU THINK YOU ARE, THE QUEEN OF ENGLAND?? I felt guilty about the privilege of it, but I also felt guilty about not taking it on ourselves out of principle. Should we be planning to pawn our kid off on someone else before he was even born? Yes, Mike argued. He cited the need to "be awake" and "to function" as reasons this hire was a necessity. Of course, the only way to deal with this decision was to get into a weeks-long argument about it. I couldn't shake the idea that I was a bad mother if I wasn't up to the job of taking care of my baby entirely by myself. Before you read any further, if it's not already clear to you, let me tell you that all of my ideas were very stupid!

My very brilliant, very wise obstetrician was the one who finally settled it during a checkup. When I asked her for her thoughts on hiring a night nurse, she was unequivocal. "If you can afford it, you *must*," she said. Her explanation was that humans don't raise children the way we were naturally wired to anymore. "We used to live surrounded by a village. We are not meant to raise newborns and infants without family around us. We were designed to have babies when we were fifteen and be surrounded by our still-very-young parents and grandparents and great-grandparents and cousins, who would be constantly helping us." Upon reflection, I had to accept that she had a point. That did sound better. I was already really fucking old, which meant my parents were even older than that. They were nearby in Manhattan, and while they could be relied upon for lots of love and moral support, we could certainly not ask them to stay over and change a diaper in the middle of the night. Other than them, we didn't really have available family help anywhere near us. While this is common, as my doctor explained, it definitely isn't "normal."

Mike and I still chose to bicker about this for a few more weeks, but finally, I relented. I think the kicker for me was really absorbing the fact that between the two of us we did not know ONE THING about babies. Not one. Nary a single thing about taking care of them, feeding them, swaddling them, their likes/dislikes. Maybe some help would be wise.

The third stage of the hero's journey is encountering "supernatural aid." A mystical mentor, a helper, a guide who helps usher you from your old life into your new one. An Obi-Wan, a Gandalf. (I recognize that these are all very nerdy references, and truth be told, I actually haven't seen these movies, mainly because I just personally prefer movies that are about feelings and feelings ONLY, e.g., a person has a crush on another person, a person in a small town is having a hard time with a tricky parent, a high school student must come of age by dancing! As soon as a golem or a gremlin or a gorgeous young woman with white hair down to her tush appears, I generally head to the bathroom and don't return.) When I was making my initial rough crossing into motherhood, I didn't want a wizard or a magic person or some elf queen, I just desperately needed help from women who knew exactly what the fuck they were doing, because I definitely did not.

For me, these were night nurses. Maybe it was because I was postpartum and hormonal and emotionally porous, but my experiences with each of these women impacted me profoundly. So much of new motherhood is a blur to me at this point; I can't really remember my son's first steps or the name of his first pediatrician or even his exact first words—but burned into my memory are some of the moments I shared with these women after the sun had set. They were guiding lights. I will never forget the kindness and the patience they showed me when I was at my most vulnerable.

The night nurse's job is such a contradiction. It's deeply

intimate work—being trusted to tend to a fragile, brand-new human being—and yet the term for which they work with any given family is only a few weeks, or even just days, before they are gone, and you likely never see them again. A total stranger walks into your house in the evenings and takes care of the most precious thing you have in the universe. In the standard small New York City apartment, this new person is maybe just on the other side of one wall, taking care of your baby, while you are in your bed, desperately trying to rest and recover from giving birth (and perhaps also scrolling through every social media app on your phone in an attempt to feel like you're still part of things somehow? Even though you are most definitely not).

Until you need one, you might never even know there is a whole army of women who work the night shift, usually seven p.m. until seven a.m., helping mothers handle the round-the-clock schedule required of caring for newborn babies. I'm endlessly curious about what must it be like for them, constantly entering new little worlds: walking into exhausted and edgy people's homes, seeing people's odd decor, dealing with the grandparents making everyone crazy, and in general witnessing all the mishegoss of a household upended by the arrival of a new life.

Our first night nurse was Lisa, who came to us highly recommended by a friend. We interviewed her a month before Asher was born. She had a neon pink buzz cut and a confident, funny, extremely likable personality, and I immediately felt like if I put my entire life in Lisa's hands I'd both be way more successful and have more fun. We hired her to work with us for a month.

Asher's birth went smoothly enough; I went into labor early in the morning and pushed him out that evening—the whole thing, relatively speaking, was uneventful, which is one of the best adjectives you can hope for to describe a birth. I'd been terrified of these labors I'd heard about, ones that lasted days. Still, I've never been handed a situation I couldn't self-sabotage, and for the two nights we stayed in the hospital, I did not sleep one wink. Not a one. Now was this entirely my fault? No. It's hard to sleep in a hospital with all the beeping and the blankets that are really more like paper towels. Still, I have weapons-grade insomnia at the best of times, and apparently it was not going to let a full day spent squeezing a human out of my vagina make one iota of a diff.

This meant that on the morning we were supposed to go home, I had already been up for forty-eight straight hours. I remember my vision was starting to get wavy, as if I were looking across a midday desert, and I couldn't think in a straight line. I felt like I was slipping down a drain. As we prepared to check out of the hospital, Mike went to text Lisa (who'd been on standby) that the baby had arrived and was coming home and could she get to our house around seven p.m.? Because my brain had turned to melted soft serve, I stopped Mike before he pressed SEND. "Shouldn't we have her start tomorrow? To have one night at home with the baby as a family?" Mike, who'd been pretty good up to that point about absorbing all the insanity I was spewing, finally felt compelled to say something along the lines of—not exactly this, but similar to—"Shut the fuck up, you maniac."*

The process of getting from the hospital to our apartment in Brooklyn took a long time. You have to wait for security to triple-check that your baby is your baby and sign a bunch of papers legally attesting that this is REALLY your baby, then you have to wait until someone can wheelchair you out. This all took about an hour. Then we had to VERY NERVOUSLY buckle him into the car seat for the first ever time, which, given that he was a day and a half old and all of seven pounds, was as anxiety-producing as strapping a tulip into the space shuttle. More time passed. Then we had to drive home along the FDR, a stretch of urban freeway infamous for bad driving, which had never felt more like a NASCAR track than it did in that

---

* For what it's worth, while he hadn't had very much sleep on the second night either, on our first night in the hospital there'd been a full-on baby boom happening, and the hospital was out of cots, which meant he would have had to spend the night sleeping in a chair. We both thought it would be better if he grabbed a room at the closest hotel and came back early in the morning so that at least one of us could get some sleep. As it turned out, the only hotel in the neighborhood with a room available on such short notice was the Marc, which is the kind of old-school Upper East Side four-star hotel where senators like to stay. So yes, I gave birth and stayed in a hospital bed underneath one thin blanket, and Mike, who had watched me give birth (I mean, yes, he did hold my hand, but like . . . c'mon) got to sleep in a betasseled princess canopy bed. It must be said for the record I know he felt absolutely terrible about this, and I absolutely encouraged him to go stay at the hotel, but still, it warrants a footnote.

moment. Mike drove while I rode in the back, holding Asher's incomprehensibly tiny hand. The entire drive, he gripped my finger with that shocking strength babies have, looking, by far, like the calmest person in the car. At some point, it did occur to me that he might be getting hungry, or thirsty? But while we were in the car, there was no way to feed him safely. The whole ride home, door to door, was probably another ninety minutes.

The doula who had helped with the birth, Cara, met us at our apartment to make sure we were doing okay before saying her final goodbye. She was a lovely Park Slope hippie type (is there a doula who isn't?) with a sweet bedside manner. That said, when I told her about how long our trip home from the hospital had been, she gave me a very direct look. "How long has it been since you fed him?" she asked skeptically. "Um, I think four hours?" I replied innocently. I could tell she didn't love this answer. She tried to say the following words as kindly as she could while still being firm: "Okay, so you can never let that happen again." As I wigged out, she continued: "Babies need to eat every two hours at least, and really dangerous things can start to happen if you let that slip," she continued. Fighting off a heart attack, I immediately pulled off my shirt to attempt to nurse, but I wasn't sure if there was anything coming out. Cara asked me to squeeze my nipple so she could observe. The tiniest, tiniest amount of clear fluid appeared—but not much. A few molecules at best? "I see colostrum there," Cara said. If you're not familiar with colostrum, it's (allegedly) a kind of superfood pre-milk your body produces before your milk officially arrives. It can be gold or clear or apparently fully invisible? I remember having read about it toward the end of my pregnancy, and my reaction was very much *WHAT IN HOT HELL IS THIS, HOW CAN THERE BE ANOTHER THING THIS FUCKING WEIRD, WHY IS IT CALLED COLOSTRUM??????*

As I held Asher to my chest, it was impossible to tell whether he was actually getting any nutrition or not, but Cara seemed confident that as long as he was making contact with my boob he was getting something. I wished I shared her confidence, but since she had drilled into my mind that the difference between being right and wrong was potentially an unconscious/dead baby it was hard to feel great about the situation.

After an hour, Cara had to go (*How dare she leave us?* I thought, as she went to help bring another life into the world). I was physically shaking by this point, from exhaustion, from fear, from hunger, from stress. This was the moment that Lisa rang the bell. She walked into our apartment to find Mike running around trying to open all our still-boxed baby-care equipment as I sat on the couch, fully in a fugue state, holding Asher. I had never been so happy to see anyone in my life.

Mike handed her the baby, and she lifted him high in the air for a moment, like a little Simba. She looked at him, considering, and then lowered him so they were eye to eye. "Ashah," she said finally, in her Trinidadian accent. "You're a good baby." She turned to us. "It's almost time for him to go to bed. Has he eaten?" I gave my "I think?" answer, which she immediately, and properly, ignored. "Do you have any formula in the house?" she asked. Now the answer to this was yes. And the reason we had formula was not because we had bought it (even though, as I will get to in a bit, I am an ENTHUSIASTIC proponent of formula) but because apparently, the minute you register with any baby sites or leave any kind of internet cookie trail indicating you are pregnant, various formula companies start sending you boxes of the stuff for free, unsolicited. One day I opened our mailbox and a giant packet of Enfamil just fell out. Whenever another one arrived, we just threw it in a closet with the rest of the things we had no idea what to do with.

Lisa directed Mike to go find the formula and, over the next several minutes, gave us the tremendous gift of dispensing with any and all preciousness about the means by which you get a baby fed. I had never cared about "exclusively breastfeeding," but I suppose if it had occurred to me ahead of time, I might have perhaps started going down the rabbit hole about which formula company might be more nutritious or organic or whatever hoop I might have made myself jump through for no reason? But when I presented Lisa with the formula boxes and asked which brand was superior, she said, firmly enough that I sensed no further questions were necessary, "They're all the same, it doesn't matter."

It doesn't. Matter.

It. Doesn't. Matter.

It. Doesn't matter.

These three words were music to my ears. There were so many things that mattered a fucking ton. With a newborn, every moment feels like the stakes are life-and-death. Getting permission to stop hand-wringing every single decision was so freeing, so calming.

Lisa's advice was to breastfeed and then always offer some formula for what she referred to as "a top-off"—a nightcap, so to speak, to make sure he was truly satiated. As a longtime wino, I loved the sound of this. Lisa was singularly focused on the notion that a full baby was a happy baby was a baby who was sleeping longer and longer. Her reputation was as a sleep training whisperer, and she'd told us when we first met that she could get most babies to sleep through the night at eight weeks. This seemed ambitious, but I respected her swagger.

All of Lisa's principles were simple, clear, and correct. Still, in my new mom fog, the urge to make something simple complicated was always there. On the fourth or fifth night of Lisa's stay with us, Asher awoke about thirty minutes after his boob milk entrée and formula digestif. Lisa went to make him another ounce of formula, but because he had eaten just recently, I wondered if food wasn't what he needed. I suggested to Lisa that maybe what he needed was just . . . me. Good ol' ma. My extremely special and unique cuddles. Lisa gave me a look. "He's probably just still hungry," she replied. But I wasn't ready to give in to this logic yet, despite the fact that I, as a grown adult, get hungry fifteen minutes after I've eaten no matter the size of what I've just consumed. "I'll just try," I said to Lisa, who threw down an Oscar-level performance as she nodded diplomatically and said, "I understand. Mothers need to have their own experience."

In the dark, I lifted Asher out of his little bassinet and sat him on the couch. I gently stroked his forehead with my thumb and sang him the mockingbird lullaby over and over, waiting for his eyes to close. He stopped fussing, and then, as his lids got heavier, we gazed at each other, his eyes piercing right through my soul the way only baby newborn eyes can. For the first time since he arrived, I felt we were having a moment, that we were falling in love, and that he felt safest and most cared for when in my soft, nurturing arms.

Finally, his eyes closed. I stood up, moving slower than a sloth, and painstakingly put him in the crib. He was asleep. Was I a hero? Maybe just a bit.

I emerged from his bedroom and Lisa looked up from the couch. "How'd it go in there?" she asked, deadpan.

"Really, really good," I replied. "He just needed a mama snuggle." At this exact moment, Asher began crying again, loudly. Lisa stood up. "Maybe we should try feeding him," she said.

In hindsight, Asher and Lisa were very much on the same page, which was that he was hungry and that I was being a true idiot. We gave him a little more formula and he fell asleep instantly. But of course.

Could you take a moment, wherever you are, to raise a glass to Lisa? To Lisa, but also to all the other women around the world who stay up all night helping these new babies survive their new mothers. Cheers to Lisa, to her patience, to her generosity in toeing the line between letting my dumbass self learn lessons the way I needed to, and stepping in to keep my son alive.

At the end of her month with us, Lisa had to go start another job, so we enlisted a night nurse agency. The first person they sent us was Janet. Vibe-wise, Janet was the opposite of Lisa. She had an incredibly calm, almost stoned presence—which I was not mad at. The same week Janet arrived, we realized that Asher was almost a month old and had still not been given a proper bath. We had attempted one, with a little plastic infant tub that fit in the sink. On one side it had a "too hot/ too cold" indicator sticker, which Mike and I took extremely literally; we agonized over getting the little dial to be at exactly the Goldilocks "just right" spot. No matter how perfectly we modulated the temperature, however, Asher started screaming bloody murder the minute we put him in the water, and did not stop until he'd been taken out and fully dried. We always panicked and ended up giving him a very insufficient sponging. For a few weeks, we felt okay skipping his bath, but after a month we really started to feel that someone who shit himself multiple times daily, and also who not four weeks ago had been "born," should probably be bathed.

When we told Janet that Asher loathed the water, she told us she was going to do a "Janet bath." I didn't know what she could possibly do differently than us, given that we were obviously perfect, but I was interested to learn. I ran the faucet and got the tub indicator sticker to make its "ideal temp" smiley face. Janet put her hand in the water and looked at me, bemused. "This water is way too cold," she said. "But the sticker," I muttered, as I put my hand in the tub and realized that, indeed, the water was an absolutely repugnant cool-leaning lukewarm. I mean, it was genuinely a temperature no human being, baby, child, teenager, or adult would ever want to bathe in. We'd been so scared of burning our son that we'd accidentally frozen him. "You also could put a bit more water in the tub," she gently suggested. Oh, right. We had also been scared of drowning him even though we held him the whole time. So basically we'd had it set up so the water was cold enough to make him shiver, and then almost his entire torso was exposed to the air. A dream scenario!

Oops.

WELP. Seemed like it was time to hand over the reins entirely to Janet. She dumped out the water and started over, and when the tub was full, she asked us for a hairbrush, a rinsing cup, and two towels. I don't know why she would need a brush (even though, just to brag, he did have a gorgeous full head of hair at birth), but I remembered that someone actually had given us a little baby hygiene kit that contained a tiny little white baby hairbrush. Someone had also given us a whale-shaped plastic rinser, and I scurried to get it from the messy pile of baby gifts that was sitting in our closet, waiting for a competent adult to come get them.

When everything was set up, she took off Asher's diaper and onesie and held his whole tiny body with one hand, as if he were a kitten, and then slowly lowered him into the water. Asher looked skeptical until his feet touched the water, and then I could see a look of pleasant surprise on his four-week-old face. Janet spoke in calm, low tones, "That's nice, huh? A little spa baby?" She moved her hand slowly over to the faucet, as if she herself were underwater, and turned on a gentle stream of (perfectly warm) water, which she poured gently on

his forehead, tilting him back and letting it wash over the back
of his head. At this point, Asher closed his eyes, luxuriating
in the feeling of warmth as well as the safe feeling that once
again he was under the care of anyone other than his dumbwit
parents.

After a few minutes of this, Janet took him out of the bath.
The time from being in the water to being perfectly wrapped
in a towel was less than a millisecond. She carried him into his
room where she dressed him in his onesie, and then swaddled
him in a blanket. She put him on her lap, his head at her knees,
and began to slowly, lovingly, brush his hair, at which point he
seemed to achieve a state of bliss that I, as his mother, had never
been able to evoke. I took a video of this moment. The moment
she starts brushing, he closes his eyes. "Sloooow motion, we
have lots of beautiful hair, young man," she murmurs, and then,
he smiles one of his very first full smiles. It is so beautiful. It's
not just because he's beautiful and I'm his mom and I think he's
beautiful; it's the magic of seeing this tiny, new creature experiencing such pure, innocent pleasure for the first time. He makes
little coos of joy as the brush goes back over his crown. Watching
this video while writing this, I had forgotten that you can hear a
dumbfounded me just out of frame, laughing as I watched in awe.

Please raise a glass to Janet. May we all be so lucky as to one
day receive a Janet bath.

After two weeks with us, Janet had been booked to start another job, and so we were back to the agency. This time they
sent us Vivian.

I loved Vivian from the moment she walked in the door. She was soft-spoken, and had a quiet, still-waters-run-deep energy. She said very little, but whenever I occasionally made her smile or laugh, I felt like I'd won a million dollars. And there was something about the way she held my son, from the first moment I introduced them, that touched me. She wasn't just gentle, she was tender. She would take Asher in her arms and look deep into his baby eyes. It was the tenderness of someone who, I sensed, perhaps needed a bit more tenderness in her own life.

After dinner, Vivian was always ready to slip quietly into Asher's room to begin her overnight watch, but I was lonely and occasionally lured her with dessert into the living room, where we would page through my trashy magazines and talk about what shoes we would wear and which starlets were dating the absolutely wrong guy. Gradually, Vivian told me a little bit about her life. Her adult daughter had breast cancer and she was helping take care of her. Vivian went to church every Sunday. She had blackout curtains in her bedroom to help her sleep during the day, but still, she said she often didn't get more than four hours of sleep in a twenty-four-hour cycle. "It's enough," she said.

Vivian's time with us coincided with the first trip Mike had to take out of town for work. Even though he was only going to be gone a few days, I was deeply grateful that I still had another person to help at night. It wasn't even so much about sleep (I mean, it was, but I'd had the decimating realization that even with the night nurse actually feeding the baby, I still had to wake up in the middle of the night to pump anyway; again, devastating information) as it was that I was still a scared, inexperienced new mother, terrified of being alone with my baby. Although perhaps more accurately, I was scared of my baby being left alone with me, seeing as how I was clearly NOT GOOD AT THIS.

On the first day Mike was gone, our nanny left at five, as usual. (Have I mentioned we were employing a full-time nanny? I know, I know. It's a wild amount of privilege that allows you to pay to build a village, but without paying for this village, we would have had no village whatsoever.) Asher was smiley and sweet as our nanny left—he was always in a good mood when he was with her, because she was amazing—and his happy mood continued for about ten minutes. But then, as the sun started to set, he began to fuss. Fussing turned to crying. And finally, crying turned to screaming. We had entered that strange time known as the witching hour, when babies lose their shit and will not stop crying no matter what you do. His screams were urgent, alarming, the kind of scream that you start to worry will prompt a neighbor to call the police. I tried everything—he was changed, he was fed, it wasn't too hot, it wasn't too cold, nothing on him was too tight. I held him, rocked him, put him on the floor, danced him around, sat with him, and still he screamed. In fact, the more I tried to calm him, the more agitated he became. His main problem seemed to be that I was his mother, and frankly, I agreed. That of all the women in the world who could have been the recipient of this great little soul, he had somehow been beamed to the dippiest of dip-shits. At some point during the second straight hour of crying, I started to cry.

Finally, Vivian walked into the apartment at seven, to find both the baby and me freaking the fuck out. I was embarrassed and exhausted and angry. "He won't stop crying!" I yelped like a full lunatic, as I handed him to Vivian. She'd barely had time to take her jacket off and wash her hands. Even now, I remember how she encircled him in her arms, how she didn't say a word. She looked him in the eyes and swayed, just barely. I remember there was a bright patch of setting sunlight on the wall just behind her as we stood in his room, and even though she was holding him, for the first time in hours, I felt held, like someone had me, someone got me. In ten seconds, he completely calmed down and wasn't making a peep, just looking back at her as soulfully as she was looking at him. A beautiful quiet filled the room, as if a conductor had just concluded a symphony.

I was agog. "How did you do that?"

Vivian gave me a reassuring smile. "Sometimes it's just, you know, change of hands."

That's all she said.

Change of hands.

Just three little words, but they have stuck with me all of these years. It's such a simple thought, but it's among the very best advice I ever received about being a mother. It is not just great mom advice, but great life advice. Sometimes we are too close. Sometimes our creativity, our relationship, our book, our project, this thing we are working so hard on, needs space from us. It's okay, sometimes, to not just ask for help, but to acknowledge that in fact help might be the only answer. The truth is, there will be times where you actually must step away from what you love in order to love it right, when your absence might be more helpful than your presence. There will be times when in fact the right thing to do is to say, "I need a break." Unfortunately, we live in a culture that philosophically does not believe in the notion of mothers needing a break, and, as a result, doesn't invest politically or economically in making breaks possible. There is an excess of mom-wine-drinking jokes and poop-on-the-clothes-at-work jokes and a lot of judging jokes about bad mothering. But none of these things afford mothers, who are literally carrying humanity forward around their necks, the simple grace of a change of hands.

When you have a child, there are so many people you meet who are in your life for just a fleeting moment, but they are forever tied to your passage into parenthood. I think about Vivian all the time. I wonder where she is, what she's doing right now; and I hope that somehow, someday, I can be her change of hands.

Hair

Asher was pretending to give me a haircut, something he does by scraping a wide-toothed comb around my head like a rake. After stirring my hair into little knots for a minute, he said:

"Mom, I can see your brain."

It took my brain a second to realize that he meant he could see my scalp.

This is my chapter about hair loss. The process of having to sit and write anything usually fills me with dread, but I'm actually so excited to write this that I'm going to say the most important thing at the beginning, even though chronologically it probably should come later, because I DON'T WANT YOU TO WAIT FOR IT. OKAY, HERE IT COMES.

- IT IS NORMAL FOR WOMEN TO LOSE THEIR HAIR.

- YOU ARE ALLOWED TO LOSE YOUR HAIR.

- YOU ARE BEAUTIFUL WITH OR WITHOUT YOUR HAIR.

I'm excited to write it, because when I first started noticing that my hair was falling out I went on the internet in the hopes of getting some information on how to make it stop and also how to feel better while I waited for it to stop. What Google turned up first were a million articles that basically said there was almost no way to reverse hair loss, and then maybe twenty message boards specifically focused on female hair loss, all of which actually made me feel much worse. It was a very dark rabbit hole, one in which the rabbits were a ton of scared, panicked, sad women. (This is not a judgment; I was absolutely one of them.) But after spending way too much time in there, I finally had to skedaddle on out. In the absence of anything truly useful to do about my hair, I just kept wishing there was something to read that would make me feel less panicked. Something that was maybe even hopeful? And/or life-affirming or funny or even all of the above?

But after years of searching, I've never been able to find that thing. So this is me trying to write it. My hope is that maybe one day, when some anxious woman searches "female hair loss," this essay will be what autofills first (or at least before the sad chat rooms and useless articles, but probably after the sponsored ads for laser combs?). And when that beautiful lady finishes reading, she'll feel better. Because she'll have finally read something that says:

- YOU ARE ALLOWED TO LOSE YOUR HAIR.

- IT IS NORMAL FOR WOMEN TO LOSE THEIR HAIR.

- YOU ARE BEAUTIFUL WITH OR WITHOUT YOUR HAIR.

We live in a world where more women deal with hair loss than don't, and yet the world makes us feel like when this normal thing happens we have committed a CRIME. We are made to feel like we will get whisked off to the same lonely spinster body prison where women with cellulite and other deformities of the normal are left to languish.

- YOU ARE ALLOWED TO LOSE YOUR HAIR.

- IT IS NORMAL.

- EVEN FOR WOMEN!

- YOU ARE BEAUTIFUL WITH OR WITHOUT YOUR HAIR.

So here is my hair story.

15 Years Old

When I was young, I had great fucking hair: a long, thick, chocolate-brown, wavy Jewish mop. At the height of its powers, my ponytail had the girth of a Coke can. Tragically, but not surprisingly, I had no idea I had great hair. In fact, I hated it. I was a teenager and it was the late '80s and all I wanted was smooth, flat, gold Marcia Brady hair, as WASPy as Christmas itself. In fairness to me, we were all still living under the tyranny of Marcia Brady hair, even decades after she first swanned onto our televisions.

So there I was, a teenage girl, dumbly unaware of my good hair fortune, and of course only focused on what I saw as the many attributes I didn't have (e.g., boobs). Then I grew boobs, and that was briefly fun, but just a few years after they appeared, it became cool to have small boobs again, and right when I turned to my hair for comfort, it started falling out.

30 Years Old

I was dating a lovely, funny bald man. He told me that when he first noticed his hair was thinning in his twenties, he completely freaked out. He began "tracking" (his word) male celebrities he thought were trying to hide the fact that they were going bald. I don't think I'm outing Jude Law by saying Jude Law was at the very the top of his tracking list. But there were many others.

I don't remember exactly what my first moment was. I can't remember if it was the moment I noticed that my part, which I'd barely even seen before, was suddenly slightly visible, a thin little stripe of white on the top of my head. Or maybe it was noticing that there was more hair trapped in that little drain-catcher. In any case, one day, I noticed. The first thing I did when I noticed was to try not to notice. That lasted about a month before the noticing happened again, at which point it snowballed into an observation, and then the observation avalanched into fully spinning out. I called my (beloved) GP, Dr. Rahman, and made an URGENT appointment so he could tell me that this either wasn't happening, or that if it was happening, he could fix it immediately. I walked into his exam room and was surprised at just how much embarrassment I felt as I said, "I'm worried I'm losing my hair." I remember him using both hands to flatten the hair on the top of my head as he looked. My hair at this point was still fairly thick, and I kept waiting for him to say, "You're fine," but instead he said, "Of course you are," and my stomach dropped into my feet. He told me I should see a dermatologist, and then an awkward pause settled in where I could tell he knew I was spiraling, but there wasn't anything substantive left for him to say. I don't remember his exact words, but I think he said, "This is really hard for women." I can't say for sure he said that, but I'm pretty sure one of us or both of us either said it or felt it.

32 Years Old

My hair is getting thinner. I don't know how noticeable it is to others, but I see it every time I see a photo of myself or look in the mirror. Bathroom mirrors are especially harsh, as there's almost always an overhead light that shines right through my increasingly diffuse hair and highlights my visible white scalp. I get depressed. I mean, I was depressed before, true. But now this new depression is frosted on top of my preexisting depressions. My hair loss is on my mind, and my head, all the time.

Like my former boyfriend with his Jude Law list, I start tracking other women's hair. I scrutinize female celebrities who I suddenly notice are doing specifically suspicious combedover hairstyles. But mainly I just look at the tops of women's heads as I stand in the subway, inspecting the strands of every seated woman I can see. Statistics show that at least forty percent of women have hair loss. From my unscientific viewpoint on the subway, it's way more than that. Here and there I see a few lucky ladies with truly stunning manes that inspire desperate jealousy in me, but it seems like more than half have a little "brain" showing. If this is a natural process for so many of us, why has society told us we're not allowed to lose our hair? And how come men are? I mean, I knooooooow it's hard for them too, but the good news for them is once they accept it and just shave it down, pretty much every one of them looks better than they did before.*

In search of answers, I went to a dermatologist, who did a whole panel of blood tests. I was hoping they would show some nutritional deficit or hormone imbalance. I didn't want it to be anything serious, but still, HOW FUCKED UP IS IT THAT

---

* Dictionary definition of this in my mind is tennis legend Andre Agassi, who spent so many years in a bandana and a mullet, and I just want to say if anyone ever wants to talk about Agassi and his mullet, it is truly a topic I could talk about nonstop for a long brunch or even a full dinner.

I WANTED SOMETHING TO BE WRONG WITH ME?? The blood tests came back normal.

The dermatologist tells me to just use Rogaine, with one warning: "Don't bother using 'Women's' Rogaine, though—that's just marketing. Use Rogaine for men; it's fine." I go home and open my medicine cabinet and look at the three pink boxes of female Rogaine I'd already sheepishly purchased. Buying female Rogaine at the pharmacy had felt terribly humiliating. I'd tried employing the same classic college-era strategies I'd used for "hiding" condom purchases from drugstore clerks by burying them under many other nonsexual purchases, because obviously they'd never seen that trick before! Surely this person buying toilet paper and ponytail holders and ChapStick couldn't also be off having dirty sex!

I couldn't imagine now going back and having to find more crap to hide my men's Rogaine purchase.

33 Years Old

I was desperate. I tried Rogaine for about two months, spritzing my head nightly. At the end of that time, all I was left with was a sticky residue on my scalp each morning, and by making my hair look greasier, it actually made it appear even thinner. Now, in fairness to Rogaine, they're very explicit that you're not supposed to expect results before six months of use, but that was exactly six more months than I felt I could wait.

I ended up making an appointment with a "female hair loss

specialist" I found on the internet. When I arrived, everything about the office felt a little askew. First of all, there was no receptionist or any other employees of any kind. I kinda just . . . walked in. The space felt a little more like a bachelor's not-completely-clean junior one-bedroom apartment than a doctor's office. It's not like there was a bed in there or anything, but it sort of *felt* like there was a bed, if that makes sense? When the ~~doctor~~ female hair loss specialist finally appeared, I was dismayed to see that he was wearing a lab coat and cowboy boots. I don't remember much else about this visit, because the second I saw the cowboy boots I started lightly disassociating. I think I would have felt better had he been dressed either entirely as a doctor or entirely as a cowboy. On top of all this, his thinning hair was styled in a long scraggly ponytail, which didn't feel like the best ad for his particular business, or for anything?

He looked at my scalp through a special magnifying glass and told me my hair loss was most likely just genetic. Gah! Genetic. I had read that genetics was both the most common cause of hair loss, and the hardest one to treat. He sold me some very expensive potions, which he said were specially formulated by his office and contained androgens (or something?) that were "better" than Rogaine, although he could not explain how. Even though I couldn't shake the feeling that this was all bullshit, I absolutely bought them (with another sinking feeling as the doctor was the one to run my card through the reader, which didn't feel very doctor-ish?). That night in my bathroom, I squeezed the gunk that was better than Rogaine onto my head and rubbed it in. I did this for many weeks, all the while wishing I was allowed not to do this. At this point it hadn't dawned on me yet that I was allowed to do whatever I wanted.

34 Years Old

I was thirty-four when I went on a blind date with my hus band. Pretty quickly, we were spending most nights together and sharing our most intimate stories with each other. But I was keeping a big secret, which was that every night before bedtime I would sneak a little bottle out of my purse, hustle into the bathroom, put Rogaine on my head, and then sneak the little bottle back into the innermost pocket of my bag. I had run out of the cowboy-boot doctor's stuff, and when it was time to go back and buy more I had an uncomfortable feeling—a kind of apprehension that I think someone wrote a whole book about called *The Gift of Fear* (which really applies more to feeling like someone might want to murder you, but I just went ahead and decided it also applied to sensing that your "hair specialist" is a snake oil salesman selling off-brand Rogaine out of his possible first-floor apartment?), and thus I did not return. For a few months, I'd given up and done nothing at all, but then after meeting Mike it felt really important to make sure my hair stayed in place, so I went back to the Rogaine. Mike has great hair, and that made it especially hard to bear the thought of him knowing I was losing mine, but as months went by, and our relationship became more serious, and the Rogaine didn't seem to be bringing any improvement, I started to feel guilty that I should warn him of what was coming so he could leave me immediately. I remember lying on my bed in my tiny apartment staring at the ceiling, gathering the courage to call him. As I told him I had something to confess, I started to cry. There was a long silence and then he asked, "What?" in a voice that definitely indicated he was feeling his own Gift of Fear. Had I killed someone? Several someones? Finally, I told him the horrible truth, which was that I was experiencing some hair loss and was scared it might get even worse and if he wanted to bolt and never speak to me again I would understand.

35 Years Old

I am working on a TV show. It's just a few of us working in a very big and drafty loft in Brooklyn, located in a somewhat dodgy building without a cleaning staff. Day after day, we think and talk and write, and maybe around week four I start noticing that a few brown tumbleweeds seem to be rolling around the white concrete floor. Upon closer examination, I realize the tumbleweeds are actually composed of my hair, and, in fact, the entire room is covered with my strands. I start wearing a kind of droopy loose-knit navy cap all the time, the kind of thing musicians in conscious hip-hop bands wore in the '90s, in an attempt to keep my hair from floating away. I was hoping I looked like some kind of older French graduate student, which I did. I looked like an older French graduate student sitting in a sea of my own hair.

I start to despair. I track more female celebrities with thinning hair, but also look with increasing yearning at women I see (famous and otherwise) who have thick, natural manes, especially older women, gals who've held on to their hair into their sixties and seventies and eighties. I dream of being a Katharine Hepburn grande dame in a popped collar, my crowning glory piled in a messy, regal bun on my head as I stare out onto some placid retirement lake.

I have a memory from around this time of being in a cab going down Fifth Avenue on the Upper East Side. It had just started to rain as we were passing the Metropolitan Museum of Art, and a woman stepped onto the curb with her hand up to hail a taxi. She was probably about seventy. Glinting around her left ear was a dramatic gold ear climber in the shape of a snake. She was wearing a simple sleeveless black shift dress that landed just below her knee. She was stunning. Also, she was completely bald. With her arm in the air, she looked like one of the Athena statues in the museum behind her. What I remember most about her, other than the bald head and the unique gold earpiece, was her expression. She looked completely calm, completely at peace. I remember at that moment yearning to have her strength. The problem was, at thirty-five I was still too much of a coward.

39 Years Old

At thirty-nine, my hairline was getting a bit weblike. When I looked in the mirror, I tried to somehow ignore everything from my eyebrows up. At the same time, I was undergoing infertility treatments to get pregnant, some of which came with the side effect of even more hair thinning. It was a really great time!

But then, one day, magically (or the opposite of magically, because a massive amount of science was involved), I got pregnant. And with my pregnancy hormones, my hair started thickening again.

It is one of the most Alanis Morissette–ian of ironies that you get amazing, fuckable model hair at the exact moment that from the neck down your body turns into a gourd. By month four, as I looked in the mirror to see the progress of my bump, I noticed for the first time in years that my hairline was solid. Everything was now the reverse of what it had been before: From the eyebrows up, I looked like Gisele Bündchen. From the eyebrows down, I looked like a guinea pig.*

The dick punch of this is that just when your mane is at its fullest, you give birth, and then a few months after that, as your hormones reset, all the extra hair that appeared on your head, as well as some of your prepregnancy hair, falls out by the handful, sometimes in clumps. When I read about this phenomenon, somewhere in the first trimester of my pregnancy, it tinged my whole hair comeback with a bittersweet anticipatory mourning for when all of my precious new growth would once again depart.

But then my son was born. And while I did become exhausted and fragile, my hair, against all odds, miraculously

---

* Please know I say this not to be self-deprecating: my first pet was a guinea pig named Chumley, whom I LOVED, and I loved his body as well as his mind.

stayed in place. At first I couldn't believe it—I had never heard of anyone who had kept their amped-up pregnancy hair. But then a month went by, and another and another . . . and still it remained. I was so grateful my son was healthy, but if I'm being honest, I was also thrilled that when I curled my hair into a messy bun, my Goody elastic had to strain to make it around even once or twice, just like the good old days.

44 Years Old

The summer my son turned four, I turned forty-four, and I started to feel crazy. My emotions constantly hovered some-where between twitchy and furious, and I could not stop my thoughts from turning in wildly anxious circles. When I noticed that coincidentally—or not coincidentally?—my period had not come around for six months, I decided it was time to see a doctor. I'd never found a gynecologist I liked in LA; the two or three I'd tried out had all revealed an uncomfortable Hollywood streak, inevitably asking what I did for a living, and when I said I was a writer, asking if I'd worked on "anything they might know." An LA gynecologist once literally made this inquiry as she was do-ing my pap smear. It's not super comfortable to have a speculum in your vagina, but to have a speculum in your vagina, AND have to see the disappointment in your doctor's eyes when you tell them you're writing for an inconsequential sitcom they've never heard of, is a true bummer. Nevertheless, between the insane feelings and the lack of menstruation, sucking it up and getting to the lady doc seemed to be the correct move.

After doing a panel of tests, this new doctor informed me that my hormones were fluctuating between extreme highs and lows, and that this fluctuation was causing my emotional distress, as well as ovarian cysts. I was officially in perimenopause. For those who don't know, perimenopause is the phase before you're fully in menopause, where you get to freak out that you're going to be in menopause soon. It's like being engaged to menopause.

The doctor said that to control the cysts, I would have to go on hormonal birth control.

I had not gone back on the pill since giving birth, having convinced myself that this was why my hair situation had improved. I had decided to roll the dice on risking another pregnancy I really didn't want rather than risk losing the miracle pregnancy hair regrowth I wanted very much. Now, admittedly, given my age and the great trouble it had taken to get pregnant the first time, the risk was quite low. Still, was this great behavior? Oh, for sure it was not. But there was a lot of chatter on the hair-loss message boards (yes, I had returned) about a potential link between birth control pills and female hair loss, and while none of this was based on proven science, it was supported by dozens of random internet comments, which felt like . . . something? *

I told the doctor I was concerned about the pill's effect on

---

* There was also a lot of chatter about the potential link between everything and hair loss. Antidepressants. Stress. Hair dye. Fatigue. Exercise. Cake. Air.

my hair. Even though she was very nice, her vibe re: this concern was *Who cares?* This had been the attitude of pretty much every doctor with whom I had tried sharing this topic. While all of them remained polite, the undertone of every conversation was still very much *Excuse me, I'm too concerned with keeping you alive to care about your ponytail*, and in fairness how can you question that? She prescribed me a low-estrogen pill.

Within days of starting it, my mind began to quiet. The frantic, angry currents that had been jolting my brain for months began to fade. I felt better than I had in months, emotionally and physically.

But sure enough, as I was brushing my teeth before bed a few weeks later, I noticed that the sink was accented with about ten little thin lines. I took my fingers and ran them across my scalp, and when I pulled them out again, about twelve more hairs came with them.

This has gone on steadily since. Shedding and more shedding.

And yet . . .

I find myself, for the first time since this whole saga had started, not giving a shit. My first instinct is not to go online or find another fancy dermatologist who will sell me tonics. Instead, I just look in the mirror and imagine what I might look like if I just stop wringing my hands and buzz off my hair.

What is different now? I'm forty-four. A buzzed head probably would have been more flattering at twenty-two, with no dark circles under my eyes, less sun damage, ET CETERA, ET CETERA. But the asset I have now, that I did not have then, is the gift of having no more fucks left to give. Which is to say, thanks to almost five years of motherhood, I've now had a lot of practice with letting go of vanities. The indignities of being covered in snot and vomit in public, leaking boobs, a flappy stomach that just seems to hang there no matter what I do to get rid of it*: all of these things individually absolutely sucked. But when tallied together, the sacrifices I've made as a mother give me power. All the months of pretending I was invincible for the sake of a child have, in some ways at least, convinced me of the same belief. So fucking what if I'm losing my hair? SO WHAT????? (She screamed.) Maybe it was the fact that my body has already changed so much, I've become accustomed to seeing someone unfamiliar in the mirror. Maybe it's the fact that any kind of criticism about my appearance can now be met with the retort I AM BUSY KEEPING ANOTHER PERSON ALIVE. (Still screaming.) And to repeat:

IT IS NORMAL FOR WOMEN TO LOSE THEIR HAIR.

YOU ARE ALLOWED TO LOSE YOUR HAIR.

YOU ARE BEAUTIFUL WITH OR WITHOUT YOUR HAIR.

I used to lie awake at night, fretting that the loss of my hair would equal the loss of my femininity. Now I know the most

---

* To be honest, almost nothing, but still.

feminine thing in the world is self-acceptance, pride in who you are, what you've sacrificed, what you've lost, how you've fought and cried and persisted to turn your losses into gains. I think about the beautiful Athena I saw standing in the rain years ago, her hand up high. I could not imagine my way to her peace then. But I have found my way to the Land of No Fucks, and now I can see it. Further years on Earth, should I be so lucky to be blessed with them, will bring further shedding of everything that doesn't matter and really never did. I envision myself bald, in a tank top and earrings, my arms wrapped around my smiling boy.

Teddy Ruxpin

The number one bestselling toy in the country in 1985 was a bear named Teddy Ruxpin, one of the first widely available animatronic toys. Nowadays you have to pay top dollar for a quiet, hand-hewn Scandinavian toy that will just shut the fuck up; the cheaper default is some kind of talking, beeping, or screeching piece of plastic. But in the mid-'80s, Teddy Ruxpin was the apex of toy bear technology. I can remember sitting on the floor in our living room, close enough to the TV to be able to manually change the channel, as you had to do back then, when the Teddy Ruxpin ad first came on.

The pitch was as follows: a little kid goes to the front of his classroom for show-and-tell. He claims to have a bear that can talk and tell stories. The other children yawn and roll their eyes because obviously their classmate is making it up. I mean, these are clearly rude shitty kids, but we don't believe this third grader either because what the hell is he even talking about? He looks sad. Then, suddenly, we are in a CLOSE-UP on the bear's back. The teacher opens a hidden cassette player. She slides in a tape and turns a little dial. The bear's eyes pop open (nightmare), and he speaks—"Hi! My name is Teddy Ruxpin." Cut to the classroom—all of the kids' minds are blown. We cut back to the bear—"Can you and I be friends?" he coos. The kids all nod, hypnotized, as if they were in a cult (these kids are not the greatest actors, if I'm being honest). We leave the classroom as a British-ish voice-over tells us that this storytelling bear comes with an illustrated book and cassette.

Maybe you remember this bear; maybe you have blocked it out. I'm not offering you the option of having truly forgotten it. Once seen, there's no way it wouldn't haunt you, if not your waking life, then your dreams. There was something disconcertingly gothic about an inanimate toy with a moving mouth and eyes, telling a story as if it were alive.

Or at least this is what I thought before I became a mother.

When Asher was born, we were determined to read to him constantly, as recommended by the American Academy of Pediatrics and all the other societies and associations aimed at raising intelligent, successful kids, or at the very least, ones who will help take care of you when you're old.

I was the primary bedtime person and thus, by default, the primary reader. I enjoyed this task. It's deliciously snuggly, and, as an added bonus, baby books are about two words long, so reading three books takes one minute. Over time, however, the books progressed to being ten words long, and then soon enough they were twenty words long, and then they were ten pages long or longer, and that is when I first began to notice an odd phenomenon occurring. After a long day, during which my brain filled with unexpressed anxieties and petty injuries, when I finally settled into book time with my son, I magically had the ability to read an entire book out loud without ever having the slightest clue as to what I was even saying. I was doing a good job—acting out parts with different voices, really digging into characters—but the entire time my thoughts were on something completely different. I wasn't thinking about the story. I was fully on autopilot, a mouth making words, but with no one really home.

This felt REALLY FUCKING WEIRD. I used to be a human female. I was now Teddy Ruxpin.

The first time it happened I was slogging through a book about monkeys. Or maybe it was one about trucks. Monkeys or trucks, they all blend together. In any case, it was a new book. Our fiftieth book about monkeys or trucks.

These are the words I read out loud:

The Little Tow Truck loved to help his friends. He didn't know he was little.

But then I heard another voice say:

I wonder how much longer I have until I look truly old. I'm forty-four. Surely these must be the last few years of not looking fully old.

Hm, that's weird, I thought. How was I saying one thing and thinking another?

My lips continued saying something about a truck:

Little Tow Truck wanted to help his friend Excavator build a new building.

The other voice went on:

I wonder what Oscar Isaac is doing right now. I mean, like, RIGHT now. He's probably resting.

My hand turned a page. I don't know how I knew I had finished reading this page, but somehow I did? Asher was riveted. I spoke:

But Excavator said, "No thanks! My big friend Bulldozer is helping me." Little Tow Truck was sad.

As Little Tow Truck reeled from this slight, my endless inner monologue continued, untroubled and uninterrupted by anything my physical body was simultaneously spewing about trucks.

Should I buy one of those NuFace things? I don't love the idea of electrocuting my face every night, but everyone I know swears by it. Ugh maybe it's too late. But maybe it's not? Maybe I could just be one of those beautiful older women who ages gracefully and gets to be the star of a targeted Instagram campaign for some kind of ethical vegan bronzer. I want a dog. Ugh, but if I'm being real I know I'm too tired to walk it. What if I could become one of those people who wakes up at five by choice? One of those women who gets up and gets a cup of coffee and sits and types out chapters of a novel before her family is even up? And meditates and is actively grateful? But you won't, because you can't ever really feel grateful, you asshole. I wonder whatever happened to that boy Kieran I liked in seventh grade. I should look Kieran up. I remember getting his number out of the White Pages. THE WHITE PAGES. Fuck, I really am old.

On and on I went until Asher's book was done. I closed it and marveled at the fact that I had literally no idea what I had just read. I didn't know the characters, the story, how it began, or how it ended. If I'd had to take a multiple-choice reading comprehension test about the book, I would not have been able to answer a single question.

How had I bifurcated into two seemingly separate beings? One who was nurturing my son—reading, connecting, present, an earth mother, dare I say goddess?—and the other a being you might call the "real me," stewing and chewing on my own problems, mentally unmoored from the moment. My little boy was snuggled into my lap, completely unaware that we weren't sharing an experience so much as I, just like Teddy Ruxpin, was simply mimicking one.

I was shocked at my mind's—or was it more my body's?— ability to do this. And beyond the fact that I was able to do it—what did it say about me that I could? Was this yet another maternal multitasking muscle that had evolved out of Darwinian necessity, an act of nature to be marveled at? Or was I very simply a woman seeking a mental trapdoor to slip through when the activities that nourished my child weren't entertaining enough for my selfish little mind?

Back and forth my two halves went, Jekyll and Hyde–ing, arguing with each other about who was right and who was wrong, until even that conversation became my focus one night as I read *Make Way for Ducklings*:

"Mr. and Mrs. Mallard were looking for a place to live."

Why do you keep doing this? What kind of person can't even listen to one book they are reading? You're doing it right now, just zigzagging around in your own dumb little head. This is a book you loved as a child, and your son is loving it right now, and that's something you should be experiencing as a MOMENT, but instead you're just monologuing again. What's wrong with you?

Of course, being on autopilot around your child some of the time is normal. And to some degree, even our kids accept this. Every time we "play cars," for instance, Asher figures out, at some point, that my heart isn't really into "vrooming" Matchbox cars over the back of the couch (I mean, it never is). He briefly protests, but then he decides that he doesn't care if I don't like it, we're continuing anyway. And yet, for some reason, with a book laid out before us, Asher doesn't seem to know that I've checked out. I think it's his innocence of my absence that makes me feel like a cheat. I tell a story, and he dives in, and I slip out. I can seem as if I'm entirely present when in truth I have evaporated, like a little humidifier mist, up to the ceiling of the room, into the past, into memories of my mother and father reading to me. They read *Make Way for Ducklings* to me hundreds of times, this I know. Quack and Mack and Pack. I loved the sound of their voices, the repetition, the drawings, Officer Michael coming to the rescue, blowing his whistle to make traffic stop so the family could waddle across the street. It never occurred to me that while they were reading, they might have been somewhere else. But now I think they must have been. Then again, maybe that's just me projecting. They read to me about the ducks; now I read to my son about the ducks, and the past and present melt into a meditation. The story exists on the page, but it also exists in the thoughts that finally come loose from my mind after these long days while I read it aloud: remembering before I was a mother; the French fries for breakfast at Lox Around the Clock every weekend with my first boyfriend; the wants I still have. And the story also exists in writing this book, finding unexpected new chapters in the overlap of the ducks, the trucks, my son, and the nine-year-old me in 1985 who sat on the floor watching the Teddy Ruxpin commercial, desperately wishing I could have that bear.

Bad News

The other morning, while we were doing his daily asthma nebulizer sesh, Ash and I were looking for fun videos to pass the time, and we ended up watching a little documentary we found about how the Airbus is built. Asher liked looking at the big machinery, and I enjoyed learning that the Airbus campus is in Toulouse, France, and also that apparently every single person who builds the Airbus is pretty much a super-model. Who knew? Anyway, we were happily watching this little airplane video when they got to a part about how tight security is on the Airbus campus. "Only people who work at Airbus are allowed to come in," the narrator intoned, as they showed a (shockingly hot) Airbus worker presenting their ID to a guard. I thought for sure Asher would glaze over this segment, as there were no big mechanical bells or whistles to marvel at, but as usual, the thing I hoped he would miss is the exact thing he caught. "Why can only people who work there go there?" he asked.

It was seven thirty in the morning, which felt a bit early to be going into questions around some of humanity's most horrible acts. I tried my best.

"Well. They just want to make sure everyone who is there really works on building the planes." Surely that would be the end of this conversation.

"Why don't they want other people to go there? Why would anyone go who's not building planes?"

Fuckkkkkk.

"Well—they just don't want anyone to go there who might make any mischief."

Even as I am saying these words, I know they are the wrong words. These are door-opening words, not door-closing words. And of course, two seconds later, he asks:

"What kind of mischief?"

In my mind's eye, the planes hit the towers. The orange fireballs blossom. Black smoke goes miles into the sky. Twenty-six-year-old me screams and runs up to the roof to see it with my own eyes, to see if this is really happening.

I try to think of a more palatable example of plane mischief.

"Well. They don't want anyone to steal the parts of the plane."

Asher takes this in as I silently pray we are done. Also, who made this stupid fucking documentary? Why did they feel the need to include a scene of checking people's IDs? The rest of the documentary is about people welding. Have these filmmakers never heard of a fucking editor? I glance at Asher, who's thinking. Finally, he says, with conviction:

"People are really nice. I don't think anyone would steal parts of the plane."

People are really nice.

My heart breaks. I feel so proud that I have raised a boy who believes this. And yet I also feel dread at the prospect of breaking the news to him that while some people are really nice, some people are just awful, evil turds. Inevitably, he will learn—from us, from school, from the internet, from the world—just how terrible people are, and have been.

And it's not even just "other people." Asher still doesn't exactly know that the "turkey he eats" is the same as "the animal turkey." "I'm eating turkey, but not the animal turkey," he says often, because his heart is so absolutely pure and innocent. The other night, when he made this distinction again, my fuel tank of parenting lies was on E and I blurted out, "Well, the turkey we eat is the same as the turkey the animal." Asher asked, "But it has to be dead, right?" Again, I was tired, so I gave up on niceties: "Yes, someone has to kill it so it's dead." I felt bad using the word "kill," but here we are/there we were. "I guess people must feel bad for the animals," he said, kicking his feet around. "Well," I replied, feeling like a full piece of shit, "some people do feel bad for the animals and decide they don't want to eat meat." *Some people.* Of which I am not one! I tried to think of how I would explain that I do have sympathy for the animals, because I'm not a monster, but I only eat some meat occasionally, and try my best to only eat meat that's raised on a farm where they're extremely nice to the animal before they kill it? Even though I'm not sure how nice they really are? Ugh, they're probably not that nice. As I'm vowing to myself to go vegan, Asher says, "I like meat."

And we leave it there for the night.

Sometimes I think about how much bad news there is to tell my kid, the endlessly long, CVS receipt scroll of truly fucking terrible things that have happened, and I want to get under the bed and never come out. How do we tell them about all this shit? Can we just play Billy Joel's "We Didn't Start the Fire" and then open the floor for questions? The first of which should be, how is this a song that played on the radio? The second of which should be, is this song good or bad? To which the answer is, no one knows.

I suppose letting Billy Joel break all the bad news is not the best idea. But I DREAD telling my sweet little five-year-old, who still thinks people are really nice, all of the bad news. And I don't even know it all. But I know at least what you know, which we can agree I'm sure is already too fucking much.

And this is why I am filled with the DREAD. How do you even begin? Where do you start? How and where and also WHEN? How am I supposed to know what age is appropriate for what atrocity? Shouldn't there be something like an early childhood vaccine schedule for terrible news? Something that's handed to us by experts that tells us, okay, this age is when they learn about this genocide, and this is when they learn about slavery, then they should return for their booster about the

Vietnam War, then at their next visit they will hear about . . . what?

I can't even write out the whats, it's all so ghastly.

There's just too much bad news.

I mean, how are we supposed to tell them about even the most basic elements of all of this nightmare?

My husband tells me that I'm too dark, that I dwell too much on the negative. (How dare he!!!!—but also both of these things are true.) "There's a lot of beauty in the world," he says, "so why don't you try focusing on that?" My response to this is always, "I knooooooooow." I DO try to focus on these beautiful things, I swear, but I'm not responsible for the fact that once the pretty things are turned over, horrible dark little tidbits are lurking under so many of them. For instance: My son really loves music. Since he was little he has banged drums and played guitars, and from very, very early on, like many little kids (and, safe to say, most people?), he loved the Beatles. His favorite songs are "Hey Jude" and "Let It Be" and "Life Goes On." I would play them on the way to school and we would sing all the "Hey Jude" nah-nah-nah-nah-nah-nah-nahs at the top of our lungs. These have been some of my favorite moments with him, and still . . . whenever we are listening, I can't help but think: *One day he will find out that one of the Beatles was killed. One of the best ones.* (I mean they're all great, but . . .) Someone killed John Lennon. And what if Asher asks why? Ugh. Then I'll have to say, "Here's where there's more bad news. Sometimes people are mentally ill." "And what's mentally ill?" he might ask. And then I would have to explain it's when there's something going on in your brain that can make people behave in ways that aren't healthy for themselves or other people. Someone mentally ill had a gun and killed John Lennon.

And then I would have to get into the existence of guns, and explain what they are and what they are for, and that someone invented them and now our country is addicted to them.

How thin can I stretch the word "mischief"?

It's hard enough to explain death to a child. Everything dies, including, eventually, all the people we love. That's already a downer of a pill to swallow, but at least it's . . . nature? Circle of life? But then on top of that they have to learn that a certain segment of people help other people along with the dying by killing them. It's a huge bummer.

Death for us began with reading about the dinosaurs. Little kids love dinosaurs and it drove me up a wall that even the youngest kids' books about dinosaurs, books for three-year-olds, included the word "died," as in, dinosaurs are extinct, as in, they all fucking died. Couldn't we just learn about T. Rex and stegosaurus without always having to include, for children so innocent they aren't even reading yet, the dinosaurs' excruciating mass death? For a long time, I would always skip over the words "died" and "extinct" while reading because, just like with Airbus security, I didn't even want to get into it, even though I know, at some point, we will have to.

I keep thinking, *How do I tell him about the Holocaust?* About the millions of humans who were killed not by a meteor but by their neighbors? It's . . . a lot to take in.

I don't remember how my parents got into it. I was probably—seven? There was some kind of "history of the Jews" documentary on TV, the sort of thing that usually runs on the History Channel, except I know we didn't have cable, so I guess it must have been PBS, seeing as how I don't think the broadcast networks would have put "history of the Jews" on prime time. What's vivid in my memory is a shot of an empty cobblestone street in Spain. The narrator explains in a grim tone that King Ferdinand has ordered all of the Jews to get the fuck out, pronto. Over the shot of the cobblestone street, there was the echo of fleeing footsteps. I turned to my father and asked why the Jews were kicked out. I recall him saying something along the lines of—and I'm definitely paraphrasing here—the world hates the Jews and always has. I remember being confused, because I was so young, and still thought "people are really nice." Then suddenly we were up to the concentration camps, and the black-and-white footage of a bulldozer pushing hundreds of dead, emaciated bodies.

There is so much bad news.

My New York City public school education taught me about slavery ... kind of. There were textbooks with drawings of people in chains, on auction blocks. The lessons were both graphic and incomplete. Slavery was followed by lethal systemic racism, which is why our textbooks don't teach us about lethal systemic racism.

There are the many genocides that came after the Holocaust (as well as before). I remember learning about the Cambodian killing fields (in junior high, maybe?) and thinking, *Oh no . . . there's more?* And then Rwanda. I won't go into the whole list, since I'm assuming you're familiar with it? (Although, according to polls, many people don't believe they really happened. The not believing of the bad news is, in and of itself, more really depressing news.)

Mike thinks our first step should be telling Asher not about the specific horrors of human history but about the more general sadnesses. That there is killing (in general). That there is rape (in general). But which is more of a bummer? I wonder. I try to remember when I first knew that these things were things that happened in the world, and how I found out, but mostly I can't. Actually, a little bit, I do remember a sinking, confused feeling in my gut when I heard about rape, because it wasn't too long after I first heard about sex, and I was having a hard enough time wrapping my head around the idea of sex that was a choice.

None of it is great.

There is the global history I'm worried will cast the first shadows on his innocent heart, the dark things that no matter what, he must be taught so that he can prevent them from occurring in the future. But then there are the individual acts of random gore, the kinds of things that make the headlines but not the history books. Decades after the cobblestone street footage, I'm hopelessly addicted to doom-scrolling. I don't *want* to click on these horrible stories, but it's like that old game we'd play when we were kids walking home, where we tried not to step on a crack. After a while, you give up because the whole street is cracks.

My morbid little Pixar brain loves to animate disturbingly specific phrases from the news into intrusive thoughts. Sometimes these thoughts are so terrifying that, unable to fight against or flee from what now resides permanently in my mind, I just get under the blankets and freeze.

I DO NOT WANT THIS FOR MY SON.

All this and then there's still the other category of bad news. I guess as categories go, this one is the kind of box you use at the end of packing for a move, the one you dump all the odds and ends into that are still lying around. The things that go in are little, but they matter. My son does not know about falling in love and having your heart broken into pieces. He doesn't yet know about cancer. He doesn't yet know that behind those amazing Michael Jackson songs he loves so much, there is . . . well . . . the tremendous amount of bad news about Michael Jackson.

I pray that Asher has a less ruminative disposition than me, that he loves spending his time on creative pursuits and joyous, life-affirming activities. That's how he spends his time now, without any of this information sogging down his soul, making him doubt the nature of the people around him. He builds his Magna-Tile dinosaurs and lays down his wooden train tracks, belting funny little songs at the top of his lungs.

He doesn't know why anyone would want to mess with the Airbus.

I know this time will come to an end.

The balm to all the bad news is, of course, that there is still so much good news. There are so many good people, so many great people. It's been hard to remember that these last few years, with so many of the most vile humans not just coming to the surface, but actually in charge. But it's important to keep our eyes on the good. Stacey Abrams and Dan Levy and Amanda Gorman and endless others, all working so hard to keep the joy beach ball in the air.

And then there are the people whose names you didn't even know about.

I am writing this chapter, this very page, on January 30, 2021. We are almost a year into the pandemic. My parents, aged eighty and seventy-seven, are at home in New York and haven't been able to visit their only grandchild in fifteen months. The vaccine is finally here and available to people their age, but the online system through which you can find appointments is a full shit show, overwhelming for even the most tech-savvy people. I want to punch a wall when I think about how hard this must be for any elder who doesn't have family or close friends nearby to help them. My parents have family, and I still can't get it done. They don't have a car, and due to fear of COVID, they only want to go to a location they can walk to (so they don't get COVID on the way to their COVID vaccine). I refresh all the websites within strolling distance from them about one thousand times a day to no avail. The news says NYC is almost entirely out of vaccine doses.

After weeks of this, I finally throw up my hands to Facebook, asking if anyone has any leads or knowledge about getting appointments downtown. A day later, I get a note from a random acquaintance. She writes: "I'm putting you in touch with a friend who is working miracles helping eligible people get appointments."

She connects me on a message with "Dana," saying I need help. "Dana" writes back immediately, asking for my parents' address and dates of birth.

I keep putting "Dana" in quotes because the skeptical New Yorker in me, the one who has a hard time accepting that people are really nice, who's read too much bad news, can't accept that this might not be a SCAM. Why would a person be doing this? It's not like I'm giving out their Social Security numbers, but still, FOR WHAT POSSIBLE REASON WOULD SOMEONE JUST BE HELPING, I wonder.

I write back to the acquaintance who recommended Dana. "So, what's up with Dana? How do you know her?" I ask faux-innocently, even though obviously, this kind of question comes from the opposite of innocence. The friend confirms she's known Dana for decades, that Dana has gotten over a hundred appointments for people she doesn't know, and that "she's just an incredibly good human."

Reading those words helps me. I lose ninety-five percent of my suspicion that this stranger is trying to fleece vulnerable old people by pretending to help them get their COVID vaccines. And yet... there's the other five percent I can't get rid of completely. Part of me hates myself for not being able to shake this feeling even in the face of all rational evidence to the contrary. But if I take a moment to feel a bit of compassion for myself, I can understand why it's so hard. It has, after all, been four decades and then some of reading one profoundly revolting story after another. It adds up, one little piece of sadness at a time, falling like dead leaves until there is a massive leaf pile of disappointment and fury and grief and horror that you can jump into and get trapped in, lying there in the cold, not knowing how to get up or get out.

I peek at Dana's Facebook page to learn more about her. If she's scamming people, it is a long con, because she's been posting for weeks with a hashtag about getting hundreds of appointments, and there are lots of other people commenting with thank-yous and expressions of gratitude, and no one is saying, *Fuck you bitch you stole my parents' life savings.* I decide that my desperation to get my mom and dad their potentially lifesaving vaccine takes precedence over a lifetime's worth of stranger-danger instincts. I give this person I do not know my parents' names and birth dates and addresses. I give her my email to register my father, who doesn't have an email address of his own.

She writes back, "I can't make any promises, but I'll try."

Not twenty-four hours later, I wake up to a message from Dana. She's gotten both of my parents vaccine slots for the next day, and screengrabbed their confirmation emails. Above the screengrabs, she's written:

> "omg can't stop crying. I hit refresh for almost 24 hours straight. maybe it will be a good day today. so glad your parents will be ok."

That Friday, both of my parents make their way to the NYC Department of Health on Worth Street for their shots. I'm in a knot until I finally hear from both of them that it's done. As soon as I hear from my father, whose appointment is in the afternoon, I drop to my knees and start sobbing. And as I write this, I'm crying again. I'm crying because after a year of complete isolation, they're on their way to some protection against this lethal virus. I'm crying because the amount of stress and fear I've been carrying this whole last COVID year has been crushing, and the load has just been lightened by a person I don't know and have never met. I'm crying because as soon as Asher said with certainty "people are really nice," I wasn't just hit with the dread of what I must tell him; I was hit with the realization of how much I miss feeling that innocent, and how exhausting it has been to walk around, my entire adulthood, so hardened. The surgical mask everyone's been fighting about wearing? That's nothing. It's so fucking easy. It's the lugging around of cynicism and suspicion, the weight of being so wary all the time, that is deadly. I'm crying because I am so deeply thankful to Dana for helping my vulnerable mom and dad, for no reason other than the one that Asher knows, in his deepest heart, is true.

In Defense of Drinking

Let me begin by listing the things I am absolutely not advocating for. You could also say that this is a list of things I am extremely against:

- Driving drunk, ever
- Driving drunk with your kids
- Driving buzzed with your kids
- Driving buzzed, ever
- Being drunk around your kids
- Unrelated to drinking: mayonnaise

Now that that's all out of the way, I want to write something called "In Defense of Drinking." This has to be called "In Defense of Drinking" because I know I have to be defensive about it, and I have to be defensive about it because, well, you know why. Because every few years a think piece goes viral about Mom Juice culture and Mommy Drinking in which the writer wrings their hands over these bad mommies and their wine. (Not one finger was ever wrung over male authors with families who wrote entire oeuvres about drinking their dicks off all over town while their wives sat with the kids at home. Not to mention that they also drank at home! Everywhere! Anywhere they wanted! It was part of their very necessary art!) And yet—someone catches a whiff of a couple of moms having a few ounces of alcohol while taking care of their babies or toddlers or kids, and they just can't believe women would do this. The danger! The abdication of responsibility! The selfishness! Those poor children, left to fend for themselves while their mothers zone out and neglect them and from there heaven can only imagine what kind of other immoral activities—sucking who knows how many peens for loose change down by the pier.

The think piece bemoans not just the behavior of these mothers, but the numbification/trivialization/alcoholization of motherhood, which, as everyone knows, is a state of supreme sacrifice in which any pleasure can only be experienced at the expense of the child, and thus it's best if such indulgences are avoided entirely. Sadly, the think piece says, the very fact that you need to be reminded of motherhood's sanctity is yet another indicator (aside from the giant glass of poison grigio you're chugging) that you're a dustbin of a mother. Thank God (who is male) there are enough editorializers willing to pass the pen year after year to publish scolding screeds urging mothers, for fuck's sake, to put down the booze and get back to staring nonstop at the children and willing them into perfection with every molecule of your heart mind body and soul, because as everyone knows, that's how children thrive. If you must, you can take your eyes off of them for sips of water—but even then, everything in moderation.

Okay, so . . . here's the part where you probably should lie down.

Speaking just for myself:

I am a better mother because I drink.

Don't get back up too fast or you'll faint (if you're even still conscious)!

The point is, I know this for sure, in my bones. I don't know that this is true for other women, and for some it would definitely not be, but for me, it is.

Ugh. I can feel the anger of so many people, but this is my truth. And as Oprah tells us, this is where we must all live, smack-dab in the middle of our truth, and I for one do what Oprah tells me.

I learned that drinking made me a better mother extremely early on, when I was trying to breastfeed my newborn. This process, which was supposed to be the apex of my connection to another human being on this earth, turned out to be, at worst, physically excruciating, and at best, mind-numbingly boring.

Part of what was so horrifying about it was that I'd misinterpreted the information about how often newborns need to eat. I'd been told that babies need to be fed every ninety minutes (not just during the day; that's around the clock). So if you're breastfeeding, that's already a full boob dance card, especially because, as I discovered, feeding my child—getting him to focus, getting him to latch, waking him up from the constant milky dozing he would do the second he started drinking—usually took almost ninety minutes in and of itself. *Oh well*, I thought, *at least I'll get a ninety-minute break until the next feed.* That's when my lactation consultant delivered the real tit punch: the every-ninety-minutes stopwatch does not start from the end of one feeding. It starts from . . .

. . . the beginning.

I've never been great at math, but if you're supposed to feed a baby every ninety minutes from the moment they start eating, and the feeding takes ninety minutes, then you are feeding a baby every minute of every hour of every twenty-four-hour day.

If I could have fainted when I heard this news, I would have, but since I was already dead, I couldn't. I was, in a very real sense, being eaten alive. My existence revolved around a giant Styrofoam breastfeeding pillow I buckled around my waist: buckling it on and feeding the baby, then removing it for maybe a couple of minutes at a time to go pee or shit, or to change the giant pad I'd stuck to my underwear to control the heavy, clotted bleeding you deal with for over a month after giving birth.* I could not go out. I couldn't really sleep. Hormones had flooded my brain and I could not control my urge to cry. But even without the hormones, who wouldn't cry in this situation? Moreover, who wouldn't drink?

---

* You can't use a tampon or something bad will happen. They don't tell you what it is. They just look you in the eye and say don't wear one under any circumstances.

When someone has broken their leg and is walking around in a cast on crutches, no one expects them to say, *This is the happiest time of my life. What bliss, I am AMPED.* And yet society as a whole seems unwilling to acknowledge the pain of new motherhood. Sometimes it feels as if every bone in your body is broken, including the bone that is your soul, as well as your vagina bone (do vaginas have bones?). The point is, when you break a bone in the Alps, a St. Bernard brings you a jug of whiskey.* Why should motherhood be any different?

My lactation consultant had approved Guinness as a potential stimulant to my milk supply, and my beloved OB/GYN had told me drinking while breastfeeding was basically fine as long as I didn't "get blackout drunk." To be honest, blackout drunk felt like the only sufficient level that would fix how bad I felt. But at least a beer was something. I didn't have a St. Bernard, but I did have a husband, who I told to run as fast as possible to the closest bodega and buy all the Guinness that they had, and to bring it unto me upon my breastfeeding pillow.

I still remember the feeling of the brown bottle against my lips, and sucking down that cold liquid with everything I had, mimicking almost exactly what my son was doing to me, both of us desperate to fill ourselves with life. I don't know if it makes me a bad person, or a bad mother. But I do know that in that moment I was able to relax enough to genuinely enjoy my baby for maybe the first time, because in some way, I achieved a true

---

* If this isn't a real thing, DO NOT TELL ME.

sense of empathy. Magical liquids soothed us both into a kind of gentle euphoria, and our closeness bathed us in warmth. It was, actually, one of the first moments I felt like a good mother.

The mindfulness movement has become a part of our collective consciousness. I am mostly thankful for this development, as most of my habits are pretty mindless: the way I eat (I gobble my meals like they're in a trough); the way I get lost in my phone (why did I just spend an hour on @kaiagerber Instagram, is she really reading a book or just pretending to, what am I doinggggg); the way I do most things, pretty much. But after almost four years, the one area of life where I must insist on stumping for the pros of occasional mindlessness is mothering. I truly believe that on occasion—I repeat, not all the time; just sometimes—being *less* present and letting your mind wander might not be just forgivable, but actually necessary, to continue with the entire endeavor. For moms of small children, hypermindfulness is the baseline state for every single second of every day in a way that can't be abandoned for even a moment: Is my child safe? Is she about to swallow a penny? Is he cranky because he has a fever that is about to get high enough that we'll have to go to the ER in a panic? He's asleep, yay, but wait, is he breathing? Ughhhhh . . .

This level of constant attention is exhausting but, of course, vital. During those first few months, the stakes of your minute-to-minute existence are so high, and yet the emotional landscape is so monotonous. While he was a baby, I kept thinking to myself that once he was a little older and past that terrifyingly delicate stage, and we could actually talk and interact, the pressure cooker would feel less intense and we could actually just have chill HANGS, like cool bros. Maybe, I thought, once he turns three, and we get past this phase where I have to be on a constant vigil for potentially fatal loose change, my mind and body will relax out of the Wetzel Pretzel shape they're in? Just naturally? Without having to, like, imbibe anything?

Yet as any parent will tell you, while each challenging period does end, it is inevitably only replaced by another, and then another.

Right when Asher turned three, his car fixation kicked in. I never bought Asher a toy car that I can recall, but somehow, at some point, one drove into the house. He fell in love with it, and from then it was all cars all the time. I'm not a car person. And it's more than not liking them; being from Manhattan, where almost no one I knew had a car, they feel profoundly oppositional to my very identity.

But Asher wasn't just obsessed with cars.

He was obsessed with parking.

What's that, you say? He's obsessed with what?

Asher doesn't just want to play with cars. He wants to play "parking." I know you're not asking how to play parking, but buckle up because here it comes. We have to line up fifty or so Matchbox cars. Sometimes we build a little garage out of blocks, but other times just look for parking relationally to the other cars. Asher moves his car around and says he can't find parking. I move my car around and say I can't find parking either. Sometimes I mention that I see a spot, but then he tells me we can't park there. Sometimes we find parking, but then more cars come, and then even more parking must be found.

He can play this game for hours. Not minutes. Not an hour. Hours. Hours into days. Days into months we played parking.

Let me say, my son is a brilliant, incredibly sweet, funny, and gentle boy. Parking just happens to be his favorite game. We all have things we enjoy that others might not understand. Every year I absolutely have to watch the Westminster Kennel Club Dog Show on television. My husband does not understand why I like seeing dogs walk in a circle. I don't understand what there is to not like about this. Playing parking is Asher's Westminster. There are thousands of other things I'd rather play with him (dog show?), but if I am being the mother who lets him lead, who accepts his likes and wants in order to let him grow in whatever directions he chooses, then I am the mother who must play parking.

All I think about while playing parking is how soon I will be able to stop playing parking. It's the same feeling I get when I am actually trying to find parking, a primal feeling of wanting to flee. In these moments with Asher, though, I am in a kind of double pain. The parking-game pain, and the pain of knowing that this little person, who is still emotionally unsophisticated enough to love playing parking, is simultaneously emotionally attuned enough to sense that his mother, the center of his world, is unhappy in some way, and it is a mystery to him as to why.

It is in this state that I get up and pour myself some tequila over ice. After a sip or two, the part of me that resists starts to quiet, and I am able to push myself out of the way and keep parking. I keep going. I keep mothering.

I know how much vitriol these words will generate. In my last book, I wrote a chapter called "Get the Epidural" that was excerpted in the *New York Times*. While some people liked it and wrote nice comments, it made other people oddly furious. I remember several men being mad because, as they told me, this is what you're signing up for by having a kid. One guy tweeted at me about how proud he was of his wife for her natural births. (I don't know how she felt about them because, believe it or not, the wife didn't seem to have the time or inclination to tweet at a stranger?)

A glass of wine helps me. It helps me slow down and take a breath. It helps me park toy cars three hours a day every day. Not to brag, but I have a calculator on my phone, and so I know that adds up to 1,095 hours of play parking a year. It helps me because every day there are contractions of frustration, of anxiety, of wanting to yell, of giving in to yelling, of wanting to run away, of being brave when my son is scared even though I am scared, of comforting him even though I feel I have nothing to give. Drinking has been my ongoing epidural because being a mother involves, in some way, giving birth every day.

Eulogy for My Feet

Trying to be a good mother, trying to be a good person, trying to be a good wife, trying to do good work, and trying to be a healthy-ish forty-something human all at the same time is a long march toward inevitable daily failure.

There are fights to never stop fighting, and then fights to surrender.

I have surrendered my feet.

I am pretty sure at one time in my life I had normal feet. Smooth, normal feet, and maybe, if I can get braggy for just one sec, I think they may have even been slightly nicer than just normal? I mean, they weren't any kind of GREAT, to be clear. I was proud of them only insofar as I didn't have any of the common "deviations," although I hate calling them that—no bunions, no bizarrely shaped toes, no hammertoes (don't know what those are, but they sound bad), and no fallen arches (don't know what they are either, but I guess I'd know if I had them). They were just average, fine, but still I was happy that they weren't on the list of body parts I worried about.

But now here I am at forty-five and my feet are fucking awful.

You may have had to read Oscar Wilde's *The Picture of Dorian Gray* at some point in high school and if you haven't, I HIGHLY recommend you do. It's about a hot young fuckboi who sells his soul to have his portrait age instead of himself. As he lives a life of sin and excess, his actual face remains youthful while the portrait, hidden away in his attic, decays and ages like a gnarly old melting candle, the grotesque tell about his real age.

The point is, my portrait of Dorian Gray IS MY FEET. They're hidden not in an attic, but in my shoes. If you looked at everything but my feet, you'd see a person who looks about her age, I suppose, with all body parts aging at about the same rate. EXCEPT FOR MY FEET.

From the top front, I suppose, they look . . . acceptable. Underneath, however, they look like two stale scones. The skin on the pads of my big toes is scaling—scaling!—and my heels look like photos from the surface of Mars. They are cracked. They are splitting. They are dry. They are thickly calloused. They occasionally split open so badly that they bleed and hurt and I have to cover the cuts with Band-Aids. It's hard to know if this is normal because it certainly isn't featured in any magazines or on any billboards. No one is being #brave about sharing it on their #gram. I'm sorry to be reporting all of this, but also I would never lie to you, and hopefully that counts for something?

It is a mystery to me as to why my feet have devolved in

this way. It's not like I'm walking around on glass. YES, I like to wear open-toe shoes. NO, I do not often wear socks. YES, I sometimes go barefoot in my house. But—could these benign little behaviors be the only culprits? Is that really all it takes to cause this amount of destruction? Or is it just that I've reached an age where your skin doesn't regenerate like it used to?

When I first noticed this happening, about ten years ago, I panicked and went to a podiatrist. Like Michelangelo carving away all the marble that wasn't David, he hacked off all the dead skin (or so I HOPED). The process left my feet raw and bloody. He then slathered my feet with Amlactin, an over-the-counter acid-based lotion. He told me it was the only thing that would help and not to bother with anything else or I would be wasting my precious fricking time. If you're not familiar with Amlactin and would like to find it at a store, go to the lotion aisle, pass everything that looks remotely cute, and make a hard stop at the bottles whose packaging suggests they're filled with paint thinner. You've found Amlactin!

The next step was tightly swaddling my feet in the same kind of kitchen shrink wrap you use to hold a sandwich together for a trip on Amtrak. And then, lastly, he instructed me to put on a pair of medical-grade white cotton socks, which did not look amazing seeing as how I'd arrived wearing a pair of off-brand Birkenstocks. He sent me on my way with the instructions to repeat this same routine every night for . . . as long as possible, and ideally forever?

————

I hate sleeping in socks. In the middle of the night, I wake up and feel like my feet are suffocating, which is surprising because I didn't know feet could breathe, but here we are. I tried following the doctor's routine for about a week, but after seven days, it became clear to me that the process of keeping my feet from being gross felt just as gross if not grosser than my actual feet. So I gave up, but with the hope (as I was still in my thirties at the time and hope was in high supply) that what I was seeing was a temporary glitch, perhaps due to dry summer heat.

CUT TO:

Ten years later, as I warned you at the beginning, the situation is worse. And I am not helping matters. When my feet get very cracked, sometimes—and again, I do apologize, but sometimes I will obsessively pick at them while watching TV, and get excited when I am able to peel off a huge piece of my own skin. Sometimes I'll really get in a groove and pick and peel and put all the tiny pieces of dead skin in a secret pile on the floor to vacuum up later. Agh, I guess it's not a secret anymore! I know this is less-than-ideal behavior, and in fact, it's horrendous.

The other day, however, Asher and I were playing Magna-Tiles in his room. I wasn't wearing socks. In the middle of building a garage, he casually asked me, "Why do you have so many cuts on your feet?"

"Because my feet are very dry," I replied.

He reached out to touch my foot. "Your foot feels hard," he said.

That was the comment that got me.

Your foot feels *hard*.

I looked at my feet.

Jesus, I thought. I didn't like thinking about my body as "hard." Because it wasn't meant as, *Wow, you have a hard body like Jen Aniston's tush is hard*, but it's hard like, *Your body is mummifying*.

That night after I got into bed I panic-ordered pumices, a sloughing spray, more Amlactin, and multiple other acids containing moisturizers that came up in a Google search of "how to fix very bad cracked dry heels feet the worst." I also bought an acidic spray that you pump onto your feet as a prep treatment before pumicing. Over the next few days, a shocking number of boxes arrived, and it became clear in my Ambien state I had accidentally ordered a few things twice. Alas.

For a while I was all in on trying to repair the damage. I acid-sprayed, then pumiced, then moisturized, then Aquaphored, then shrink-wrapped, then night-socked. The whole process took at least twenty minutes, which, at the end of a long day, very much seemed like twenty minutes too many. It was twenty minutes more that I could be sleeping, which felt really valuable seeing as how every single morning I wake up feeling like I could have used exactly twenty minutes more sleep.

After a few weeks of intensive effort, the feet showed only the tiniest amount of improvement. Some of the skin that hadn't been that bad in the first place smoothed a bit—but the craggiest crannies remained rough as ever, like overtoasted English muffins at the ends of my legs.

And then one night as I sat on the edge of the tub spraying

my skin off again I couldn't-help-but-wonder™—why the fuck was I doing this? Would performing this ritual really help my feet get better? Or was I now stuck like this? (A question that I am finding, more and more often in middle age, comes to my mind: Is this new weird thing a today thing or a permanent thing?) More important—how much did I even care? Was this worth these precious minutes of my day when I could be trying to better myself (reading poetry??) or even worsen myself (endlessly scrolling nonsense click bait)? At least in either of those scenarios I'd be relaxing in bed.

So I decided to give up. I surrendered. I waved the white flag. These are my feet now, and this is just the way it is. It feels surreal, simply throwing in the towel on upkeeping a body part, but honestly, that's where I am. I cannot grow my son's soul and Swiffer the house and call my parents and send postcards to voters and wax my mustache and try to exercise and do my job and keep up with the news and have the half hour it takes to save my feet. Something must go, and I have decided it is them. Maybe it's because, like Dorian Gray's painting, they can be so easily hidden away. I mean, I'm in Converse at least three-quarters of the year, so no one's the wiser. But whenever I occasionally peek at how they're doing, I feel truly sorry for how I've betrayed the very feet that are taking me step by step through this life. And yet I do think that perhaps the toughening, the thickening, the hardness, is a kind of metaphysical evolution, a meeting of body and spirit around what I'm asking of my feet now that I'm in my midforties. My feet are becoming more like, dare I say, hooves? But maybe that's necessary. Everything at this stage of life is heavier now: my responsibilities, my fears, the stakes of what can and can't be controlled, and for sure, my actual body. Maybe hooves are what's needed to carry the load.

Demon Halloween

On Asher's first Halloween, he was four months old. If I had to guess the number of minutes I spent looking for his first Halloween costume, it would be about one million minutes. Why did I do this? Well, first off because I thought he would look cute as a little bear, okay? I wanted to put him in a full-body bear costume like all the other moms I saw dressing up their babies and toddlers as adorable little whimsical creatures like a bee or a lobster in a pot. He was already the fucking cutest baby in the world, but I still couldn't resist the pull of seeing his perfect little baby face looking out from a full-body animal costume.

The costume arrived. It was like a thick furry brown snowsuit made from polyester brown fur with a polyester backing. Against his objections, I mushed Asher into it. He looked at me. I took a picture. He started to wail. He had been in it for a total of two minutes. I took him out of the costume and then hung it up in his closet even though not only was he never going to wear it again, he wasn't even wearing it now.

When you become a parent, Halloween becomes your new New Year's Eve. The pressure to drunkenly make out with someone at midnight is replaced by the pressure to create the most adorable, Pinterest-worthy, candy-filled night of fun a child has ever experienced. I liked Halloween well enough as a kid, but then in my twenties, long before I became a mother, I began to loathe it. Halloween parties were as disappointing as New Year's Eve parties, but you had to put more effort into going. Why did I have to dress up to get to the drinking and making-out part? Plus, grown adults in costumes were repugnant to me. Finding men attractive in their regular clothes was hard enough; I could not handle one dressed as Borat.

In my thirties, while Mike and I were living in a Brooklyn high-rise, I found my Halloween sweet spot, which was participating as a non-costumed adult patron on behalf of the trick-or-treating youth. Every October you could sign up as a treat-friendly apartment, and then on the big night, from six to eight p.m., little kids would make their way down the building, careening through the halls. It was—there's no other way to say this—cute as fuck. There weren't that many activities that got me jazzed about imagining being a mom, but the notion of being able to hold my kid's hand on a cool fall evening, while his other hand holds a plastic pumpkin bucket filled with Hershey's miniatures for me to wolf down later, was an appealing idea.

Once I became a parent, there were so many societal expectations of parenthood I was able to shrug off as outdated or rigid—yet I could not shake my desire to create a classic, picturesque Halloween.

Asher had other ideas.

The following year, we attempted to dress him as a pumpkin. I ordered the costume off Amazon, and it was essentially an orange felt sack with a green felt stem hat. Asher reluctantly accepted the sack, but when he saw the hat he made it clear no one was to come near him with it. Without the green stem hat, though, the orange felt sack looked less like a pumpkin and more like . . . an orange felt sack? Still, a friend of ours with a son the same age as Asher was throwing a Halloween party, and we made our way there. The minute we arrived, he wanted to leave. I got one picture of him looking very upset. I added this to my ever-expanding collection of photos where he looked very upset, grabbed a handful of chocolate for myself and carried my now-crying child home. *Oh well,* I thought, shoving Snickers Minis down my gullet to soothe myself, *by next year he'll like Halloween.*

The following fall, he had just started preschool. His new little friends, mostly two- and three-year-olds, were amped for Halloween by the second week of September, and by October 1, many had already started showing up at school dressed as cows, mice, ghosts. I was a smidge disconcerted at the gap between these kids' level of enthusiasm for the holiday and Asher's, but after eating twentyish/fiftyish more Hershey's Minis my mood began to lift, and I attributed our false starts to the fact that he was just a baby the first time around and still kind of a baby the second. Surely by now, Asher would be down to clown with Halloween.

I asked him what he would like to be and he said a fireman. PERFECT, I thought, WHATEVER YOU WANT, JUST BE CUTE ON HALLOWEEN! I threw more money into the garbage and bought him a fireman costume—a red hat and the yellow reflective coat and a little plastic red fire extinguisher.

The costume arrived the day before Halloween. I excitedly went to "unbox" it with Asher, as the kids do nowadays. As soon as I removed the coat from the plastic bag, he ran out of the room. "Don't you want to just try on the hat?" I said, pretending to be making a light suggestion when in fact I was desperately begging. I found him hiding in his bedroom, at which point he ran into the kitchen. After I had—let's call it what it was—chased him around the entire house a few times, I gave in and accepted that once again, Halloween was a wash.

The next night, after Asher went to bed, I stayed awake to wait for trick-or-treaters. But we live on a quiet, slightly hidden block, so no trick-or-treaters ever showed up. I went on Facebook and scrolled through photo after photo of friends' kids out on the town. It was a never-ending parade of butterfly wings and lion manes, painted faces, and families dressed up together on a theme—all pandas, all aliens, all characters from *Breaking Bad*. Whenever I saw themed family costumes, my immediate thought was, *How the FUCK did these people get their shit so . . . together?* I zoomed in on a photo of a preschooler dressed like a ketchup bottle next to his hot dog–costumed dachshund. Mom and Dad were mustard and fries. I felt a little uncomfortable pang in my gut as I shut the computer. I continued to sit alone at our dining room table, eating out of the untouched candy trough, ruminating on if and when we would ever have a normal Halloween. Who cared if Asher didn't like Halloween?

Me, apparently. I fucking did.

Maybe it wasn't the holiday. Maybe it was more just my fear of my son being so out of sync with the children around him that he wouldn't be able to make friends. I had been a lonely kid, and didn't make a single friend till I was almost ten. I couldn't figure out how to get in step, somehow, with what everyone else was doing. Working hard at multiple jobs, my parents didn't have much time for friends, so no friend-making skills were ever really modeled to us. I was shy and would usually spend recess wandering the yard by myself. For years I didn't spend Halloween trick-or-treating or throwing eggs at cars, the way you're supposed to when you're young, but with my family, watching the Greenwich Village Halloween parade from our window.

I didn't want Asher to be as isolated as I had been. No amount of Hershey's Minis, not even the Krackels, could drown the feeling that I was failing my son in this area. Wasn't I, as his mother, supposed to know why he didn't want to put on a costume? Why couldn't I soothe him?

You begin with a newborn who just needs food and diaper changes and warmth. Then they turn two and three and learn sad, mad, and happy. At four, the palette was even more complicated. There was nervous, frustrated, betrayed, enthusiastic.

Had my ability to care for him properly ended once he became a more complex person? Why wasn't I better at this?

Twelve months later, I resolved to try again. I didn't want to push too hard, so I floated the idea out to him as softly as if he were made entirely of eggshell, having learned that with my sensitive son, pretending to be completely uninterested in something myself was the best way to pique his interest. So while we were in the middle of playing trains, by which I mean I was making one of the trains talk to him, and we were having just a regular old conversation about coal and smokestacks, etc., etc., I made the train, ever so casually, say:

"Are you gonna dress up for Halloween?"

Asher (as himself) quickly responded: "I want to be a robot."

I almost died. I (as the train) responded back (again, so very relaxed, mostly uninterested—)

"Oh, that's cool. Do you want your mom to buy a costume, or do you want to make it, or—"

"I want to make it," he said firmly.

YES. I felt a wave of relief. I waited to tell Mike until Asher went to bed so he wouldn't hear me and know how much I cared:

"Asher wants to be a robot for Halloween."

Mike lit up. "Does he want us to buy—"

"HE WANTS TO MAKE IT."

We decided we would all work on it together, a family project. I set aside a big cardboard box that could fit over a human child, and Mike went to the hardware store and bought a variety of plastic red lights, odd-looking bolts, a vacuum hose, and absolutely toxic silver paint. Asher and I picked out a pair of silver glitter rubber shoes to complete his look. We were DO-ING THIS!

After a week of work, the costume was finished and ready for a dress rehearsal. The result was decidedly . . . lo-fi. We'd painted the box with the silver poison paint, cut a big hole for Asher's head in the top of the box, and made two armholes on the sides.

Asher gingerly let us put it over his head, and then walked awkwardly around the dining room table. We hadn't been able to figure out how to cushion the rims of the holes at all, so his neck and shoulders were rubbed by raw-edged cardboard when he moved. Mike said that while this wasn't ideal, it was fine for one evening. Was it? WELP, it would have to be, since neither of us had the skill to fix it. Asher looked extremely uncomfortable.

Mike and I glanced at each other nervously. The whole situation seemed like it might blow up. Then Asher turned to us and said, "Beep boop."

My son was a robot. I was so, so proud.

Our big debut was going to be a public trick-or-treat zone on a retail block in an adjacent neighborhood, where every shop would be offering ample treats for young tricksters, starting at the very spooky hour of three p.m. on October 31. Two days beforehand, Mike found out he wouldn't be able to get off work, so it would be just Ash and me. I was a little nervous about how this would go, but Asher had started sleeping with his costume right next to his bed, and that seemed like a good sign seeing as how I keep my cell phone right next to my pillow, and it's my favorite thing in the world.

For kids who grow up on the East Coast, the collective young Halloween nightmare is that it will be so cold that you need to wear a jacket, covering your costume and ruining everything. What I did not anticipate was that the chilly version of the nightmare paled in comparison to the late-October climate-change hellscape of Los Angeles. The temperature was in the nineties when we set out in the car, Asher in his little silver shoes, and the robot costume in the trunk because he could not be strapped into his seat with it on. I cranked the AC and we headed out.

When we arrived at our destination, I deposited Asher on the baking-hot sidewalk. "You ready?" I asked. He nodded. I slipped the robot box over his head and held my breath. He looked at me expectantly. There was nothing left to do but walk the three blocks to Glendale's finest shopping district and be a perfect mother and child, perfectly, adorably celebrating the most American of fall customs. As we walked, a woman walked by and smiled at the sight of Asher toddling along, the cardboard scraping into his neck. We'd won. We'd won Halloween because a stranger thought my kid was cute in his robot costume.

We successfully waddled to the strip. The first shop on the corner was a nondescript little takeaway café. I had walked Asher through the beats of trick-or-treating many times: the code words you must say to get the candy ("trick or treat"), which will be followed by the offering of candy, which must be responded to by taking one politely appropriate piece (or maybe two, c'mon, this is supposed to be fun). We had practiced at home, multiple times.

Beep boop.

I held Asher's hand as we walked in. A sweet young woman was at the counter behind a full, dare I say overflowing, candy bowl. We were clearly among the very first to arrive.

"OH, HI," someone way too thirsty said. Oopsie, it was me.

"Hello, who do we have here?" she said sweetly.

Asher hesitated and said nothing.

She reached into the bowl and offered him a lollipop, arm outstretched.

"Happy Halloween," she said, like a monster who didn't know SHE'D GONE OFF SCRIPT. Bitch, you were supposed to wait for him to say TRICK OR TREAT BEFORE YOU OFFER THE CANDY.

Asher held the candy for a moment, and then threw it against the wall. He lost his mind. He started screaming, truly screaming bloody murder, and tore for the exit. The woman was shocked, upset. She clearly had never seen a child so furious at being handed candy, and frankly neither had I. "It's not your fault," I said, as I tried to calm Asher, who was about to break through the glass door to escape. I stooped to pick up the candy as we ran away.

We made it out onto the sidewalk. My son seemed possessed, à la the kid in *The Exorcist*; he was physically shaking, and not crying so much as roaring with rage and fear. "TAKE

IT OFF," he roared, his face blood red, and I took his costume off, my own hands now trembling. Other families were starting to go by, everyone smiling (until they saw us). Ninjas, Elsas, Annas, Moanas. The only kids who weren't smiling were the ones who looked like LeBron before a playoff game. Pure focus and anticipation.

"I WANT TO GO HOME," Asher screamed. We had been out of the car for all of ten minutes; how could we go home, after all the work we'd done on the costume? "Asher," I said. "It's okay. It's okay."

"THROW AWAY THE CANDY," he screamed.

Wut?

"THROW IT AWAY!!!" He started frantically reaching into my pocket, where I had stuck the candy, and when I wouldn't give it to him, he started whaling on me with his fists.

I had, occasionally, seen versions of reactive behavior with him before; when taken by surprise, even by a positive thing, like a balloon or a cupcake or a toy, he would want to destroy it. One holiday, my mother had very kindly given him a little T-shirt, and as soon as he unwrapped it and saw what it was, he tossed it into the fireplace (it wasn't lit but still this was a lot of drama). But never, even at his worst moments, had I seen him at this level of sustained frantic intensity.

Young revelers and their parents were now streaming past us by the hundreds. There were plenty of other kids dressed as robots walking by, many with flashing lights and complicated wiring that seemed as if it could only have been completed by someone with a degree from MIT. I was crouched on the sidewalk beside Asher, who I could not get to sit on my lap, and next to us, on the ground, was his costume.

And then this happened:

A man and his young son, both dressed like stormtroopers, were walking by us, the father unwrapping a piece of gum. As he passed, he took the gum wrapper and threw it directly into the head hole of Asher's costume. White-hot rage overtook my entire being. Was this motherfucker making FUN of us?

"What the hell?" I barked at him. I was covered in sweat and ready to maim. He looked first at me, perplexed, and then at my hysterical screaming son, and then back at the costume. His eyes widened with genuine embarrassment.

"I'm so, so sorry," he said, pointing to the silver box. "I thought that was a garbage can." He and his son hustled away.

He thought. Our robot costume. Looked like. A garbage can.

As soon as he said it, I could see it. It was rectangular and gray and had a hole in the top.

I had accidentally dressed my child like . . . the trash.

I died a million deaths.

I scooped up Asher and our cardboard garbage costume and carried them both back to the car. We drove away from Halloween, Asher's breath still hitching from his *Exorcist* moment. *I AM THE TRASH*, I yelled at myself, as I stepped on the gas. I'm a trashy little trash heap of a mom and the reason I know that is because my trashy secret is that I almost never even feel like a mom; being a mother has never stopped feeling to me a little bit like dress-up, with Asher's very existence as my perpetual costume.

The October of the following year, Asher transferred to a new preschool. He loved it, we loved it, everything was great. And then, inevitably, midmonth, the school sent an email outlining their Halloween parade plan, in which all the kids and parents were invited to dress up and march around the block in costumes. He had only been attending the school for two weeks. What the fuck was I supposed to do with this?? I fretted to Mike: Should Asher just stay home from school that day? Mike told me not to be insane. I told him that maybe he shouldn't be the person weighing in on my sanity when he had entirely missed trying to keep our child from hitting himself as a stormtrooper threw a piece of trash into his costume.

Mike thought we should ask Asher what he wanted to do.

I had another casual conversation with Asher, this time with both of us "talking as" stuffed monkeys. Gotta keep it casual, casual.

"Do you know your school is doing a Halloween parade where everyone is gonna wear their costumes?" my monkey said, looking at nothing in particular.

"I don't go to school," said Asher's monkey. "Asher goes to school."

"Yeah, right, that's what I meant," my monkey replied. I caught Asher's eye by accident.

"Do I have to wear a costume?" Asher asked me (not as monkeys).

"No. You don't have to," I replied, already thinking about how much Xanax I would take as soon as these monkeys were done talking.

Asher thought for a second. "Maybe I'll be the robot again."

You might be thinking, No. There's no way they still had the robot costume. Well you better lie down because guess who saved it and put it on a shelf next to the old infant bear costume? I mean, who doesn't keep all of their emotionally triggering failed Halloween getups in the back of their closet?

On October 31, we drove Asher to school with his costume, once again, in the trunk. Most of the kids were already in their holiday garb. I put the box outside his cubby as I urgently flagged down one of his teachers. "Asher probably isn't gonna wear his costume," I whisper-screamed in her ear. "Don't take it personally." "Okay," Sharon said, with that calm voice teachers use when they have to talk to parents who think they're successfully hiding that they're having a nervous breakdown. I went outside to wait by the gate for the procession to begin. More and more kids, little ladybugs and ghosts and rainbows, streamed into school with their parents, buzzing with Studio-54-coke-bump levels of excitement. I tried to peek into Asher's classroom, but one kid was dressed as a stop sign and I couldn't see over his head.

And then, at nine a.m. on the dot, the children were led by their teachers out to the front, one class at a time. Asher's class was last. I held my breath and kept silently repeating to myself, *It's okay if he doesn't do this. We are where we are.*

And suddenly, there he was, my little robot, walking happily, if a bit awkwardly, hand in hand with another boy, Henry, who was dressed as a butterfly. He saw me and waved.

Beep boop.

My heart swelled a gadillion sizes.

As we walked around the block in a throng of other kids and parents, I could tell Asher felt so proud. It was his first parade. He was in it, marching, a part of things, chattering happily with his friends. The other parents and I walked alongside our kids, trying to find enough small talk to fill a very long, slow procession. It was impossible not to look backward at my old ghosts and worry that they could haunt my son at any moment. But Asher's hand held mine loosely, calmly, and I let him lead the way.

Little Books

Asher has always been extremely wary of new things. I suspect this can probably be traced directly to my pessimistic little genes, although it's impossible to say how much of his inborn skepticism exists due to cosmic chance, and how much is inherited Jewish trauma. Whatever the cause, it's been in there since he was a newborn. He's always had a hard time flowing into new situations. He was happy on the changing table, and happy crawling on the floor, but the journey from one place to another caused an outsized amount of angst. Being in a onesie was okay, and being naked was okay, but the time it took for the onesie to go off or on was usually filled with screams.

Asher's aversion to transitions continued into toddlerhood. Other kids could jump right into playdates; he would always cling to me for at least twenty minutes before he could settle in. And he was very clear that me leaving his line of sight for more than an eighth of a second was strictly verboten. Violations of this rule, even for quick runs to the bathroom, were rewarded with tears, a light punch to my crotch (height-wise, this is where he could reach, so it's not as terrible as it sounds, although also, it was?), or both.

Truthfully though, I don't really like transitions either.

When Asher was two, we bought a house a few blocks from the one we'd been renting since he was an infant. I thought about my son's entire little world turning upside down. Given that I found moving overwhelming, I fretted over how overwhelming he would find it. I felt more overwhelmed just thinking about it.

I decided to talk to our preschool director, Sarah, who was always generous with developmental advice. I explained how difficult transitions were for him, even though she was already well aware because his transition into school had required either Mike, our nanny, or me to attend school with him for the entire first month, training him to adjust by leaving him one minute earlier each day.

"I think you should try making him a little book," she said.

She explained that for young kids, making a little book before an event or a change that breaks down "what's going to happen" into simple, digestible chunks is a really useful tool.

"How simple?" I asked.

"Very, very simple," she responded.

I tried to take her advice. I sloppily stapled a few pages of blank paper together into a little book. Before committing to putting words in marker, I thoughtfully typed out a draft to share with Sarah for her approval. It was a couple of Microsoft

Word pages long about everything Asher would need to know about moving, with details of the process and a lot of what, in retrospect, were my feelings about all of it. I emailed it to Sarah, who promptly responded as politely as possible with a message that was essentially, *Ummmm, not this.* She offered to write this one for me (probably sensing my complete incompetence) and asked me for a couple of photos of our family.

The next day she sent back a printable PowerPoint that read as follows: "My family is moving to a new house. Some things will be the same, and some things will be different. I will have my same crib and my same toys, but I will be in a new room. I can't wait to play with my mom and dad in my new house!!"

That was it. That was the book.

I was shocked that it was this simple. Didn't it need more? And how far in advance should I read it to him?

"It does not need more," Sarah said. "And you can share it with him maybe three days before you move. Kids don't think that far into the future. Don't tell him too soon."

But didn't he need to worry about it for longer? (I didn't say this out loud but I thought it.)

I told her that part of our plan for move day was that the movers would arrive right after Asher went to school, so by the time his day was over, he'd come back to the new house.

"Does Asher need to come to the old house after school to say goodbye?" I asked, like a full fucking idiot. "No," she said, giving me a moment to realize that my lifelong moving ritual of staring mournfully around the home I was leaving, then leaning my head against the door frame for about ten minutes, thanking it for everything it's given me before walking out for the last time, might not be what a child needs or wants.

Three days before our move, as we settled in for our bedtime reading ritual, I pulled out the little book. I steeled myself for tears, a million questions, deep thoughts, rage, processing.

I read the book. It took one minute. He looked at me.

"Do you have any questions?" I asked.

"Let's read another book," he said.

And that WAS IT.

We moved. The book somehow worked its magic because the day we moved in he seemed pretty much . . . unfazed? Or at the very least he didn't need to drink booze the entire day to take the edge off like some people we know?*

This is how I discovered that the secret to life is little books.

Over the last few years, I've now written many. And what began as an exercise in parenting my child ended up becoming something closer to a meditation challenge for me: take any potentially anxiety-provoking situation, and imagine explaining it via the most calming haiku possible. In the process of grappling with what is making my son anxious, I get down to the nitty-gritty of what is making me anxious. And in trying to

---

* me

242

think of what might make him feel calm, I'm forced to explore what, if anything, after all these years (decades?), might take the edge off of my own endless anxiety. I have to adopt a different authorial voice: What would I sound like if I were a naturally tranquil human being? The answer, for better or worse, is "not like myself." This is one of the reasons that being a parent (for me) feels like constantly being in some kind of ill-fitting drag. So much of parenting is adhering, as often as possible, to the persona of a steady, measured, self-confident, unafraid person. I am so infrequently able to do this—or even to feel this. At least with the little books, and the amount of prep they require, I have the time and space to really get into the character of someone who truly believes things will be okay.

I also decided at some point to add drawings to my little books, instead of including photos. Mainly because my printer is usually out of ink? But also because, as I agonized over details, drawing forced me to slow down. The creation of each little book is a miniature emotional journey. Some are just lightly bumpy; some are fully turbulent. No matter what the conditions, I pour my soul into these books.

There was the book I wrote when Asher was three about getting on an airplane. All the airlines have a rule that once a child is two, they cannot sit in an adult's lap, and they must be in their own seat at takeoff and landing. We had to take a flight right after Asher's second birthday, before which Mike told me ominously about a work trip he'd been on where he actually saw a mom straight-up removed from the plane before takeoff because she could not get her three-year-old child to sit in his own seat. I told him that if Asher was sitting next to me, I really believed he'd be fine. I know I've said this several times throughout this book, but it bears repeating: I was an idiot.

After we settled onto the plane, I could not, for the life of me, get him to sit in his own seat. He clung to me, full panicky baby koala. The more I tried to separate us, the more distressed he became. The plane started taxiing, and I began sweating profusely. The flight attendant came over and asked if I could get him in his seat. I said I didn't think so. "How old is he?" she asked. And then—I am not proud of this—I baldly LIED, like a lying little liar. I said he was "twenty-two months." This was very dumb seeing as she could have easily checked and tooootally busted me, and I think we all know if there's one thing flight attendants hate, it's people and their bullshit NON-SENSE. But she didn't check. Was this kindness on her part? Luck? White privilege? Most likely a mix of all of the above.

A year later, we were preparing for another flight east to visit our parents. I would wake up in the middle of the night, thinking of the mother who'd been booted off the plane. The idea of having to cancel so many plans, disappoint the grand-parents . . . I couldn't fucking take it. I started making a new little book like my life depended on it.

The book read as follows:

"We are going to take a plane ride to NYC! The airport is big and it is fun to see the planes and the trucks that help them from the window. When we take off there will be some fun little bumps but we will get to see clouds out the window! When we land we will all get off the plane together and take a car to our hotel."

I added illustrations of us all getting in the car, and then of us approaching the ticket counter at JetBlue. I had developed a shorthand for drawing our family. Asher is a smiling little boy with a bowl cut. Mike is a square-jawed man with glasses. I draw Lucy, our nanny, with a smile and a ponytail. I'm a little oval face with glasses and a wild scribble of hair—kind of like John Lennon's famous doodle of himself, but less whimsical and more unhinged.

As someone who in order to fly has to take a horse's dose of Xanax and drink wine nonstop from the moment I arrive at the airport till the moment I deplane, this was not an easy little book to write. I had to use basically the same amount of drugs to draw the plane as I do to fly in it.

Just like with the move book, Asher was interested when I offered to read it to him. And when I finished, he was utterly, completely unperturbed. In this situation, however, the real payoff would not be clear until we were butts in seats, flying.

I do hate to throw around a spoiler alert, but not only did he fly—SPOILER ALERT: HE GOT HIS WINGS. I didn't even know they gave those out anymore, but THAT IS HOW WELL THE BOOK WORKED! And look, it was JetBlue and the wings weren't a pin like when I was a kid, they were a just a puffy sticker, but we saved that sticker in a little box and I know exactly where it is and we will have it forever.

The success of my first little book ("Moving") had felt like luck—but with the victory of this follow-up ("Planes"), I truly felt like a wizard. I don't know if there's a German word for "parenting orgasm," and there probably shouldn't be because the words don't go super well together but you get what I mean. I was all in on little books.

Of course, as he grew older, the little books became more complicated. The rhythms of toddlerhood, in their repetitive simplicity, give way to a more layered life, as well as the unexpected.

When Asher was four, I noticed that he seemed to be drooling more than usual. He'd always been a drooler and I'd taken to outfitting him with jaunty little bibs, but as other kids seemed to be outgrowing this habit, I continued to see little wet dribbles falling onto his drawings. We took him to a pediatric ENT, who poked a camera up his nose and told us he should probably have his adenoids taken out. I didn't even know what adenoids were, but apparently they're some kind of tonsil-adjacent unnecessary body part, and his were swollen, forcing him to mouth-breathe. It was not urgent, the very kind and patient doctor said, but over time, the effort to be properly oxygenated could take a bit of a developmental and physical toll. As one might expect from only being able to half breathe all the time. The surgery to remove adenoids is both common and outpatient, he assured us, but it did require that Asher go under general anesthesia.

He was four, and Mike and I didn't want him going under anything. Still, after weeks of way too much googling, we resigned ourselves to the fact that the surgery needed to happen. I called the scheduler, fighting off a light heart attack.

Two months later, I set to work on the little book.

"On Tuesday we are going to go to Dr. Liu, the funny nose doctor,* so he can do surgery on your nose and help you not be so sniffly all the time. We will all go together. We'll say hi to him and then he will take you to a special room where he'll give you a special medicine that will make you sleep for a little while."

I drew Asher lying down on a little table with a smile on his face.

"When you wake up, Mom and Dad will be right there to take you home and we will eat chocolate ice cream."

I read this book to him three days before the surgery. He absorbed the information, once again, magically untroubled. After a bit more conversation in which we shared our mutual appreciation of Dr. Liu's unique comedic talents, we moved on.

The part I did not write into the little book was the part where my body was in an endless knot thinking of the moment

---

* Dr. Liu has a perfect sense of humor for little kids. The first time they met, he asked Asher if he could look at the "boogies" up his nose and Asher cracked up laughing, and forever after in our house we talked about Dr. Liu like he was Richard Pryor.

where we would take him to change into his hospital gown and then would have to hand him over to Dr. Liu. He could now un-koala himself from me on a plane, but I could not fathom how we would leave him with a stranger to walk down a cold, scary hospital hallway into an operating theater. The thought of him being frightened and screaming for me, perhaps having to be held down before going under, was too much for me to take. I called the office to ask how they usually handled the separation moment. "If you think your child might be extra anxious," they said, "we can give him a dose of a tranquilizing syrup while he's still with you." I said I figured it couldn't hurt to get the syrup while internally I screamed, *OF COURSE WE WANT THE TRANQUILIZING SYRUP, SIGN US BOTH UP FOR THE FUCKING SYRUP.*

The morning of the surgery, we got up at four thirty a.m. to arrive at the hospital four hours before our scheduled procedure time, as instructed. Asher had had nothing to eat or drink since midnight, also as instructed. I was prepared for him to start to get hungry and cranky, but miraculously, he did not. We went to the gift shop and he picked out *Car and Driver* magazine, which he thumbed through while I kept picturing the images in the little book, and visualizing the chocolate ice cream we would all eat when we got home. When our name was finally called, we followed the nurse to the changing room. Asher got in his little gown and socks, and then Dr. Liu and the anesthesiologist came in to say hello. Dr. Liu left us the syrup dose in a little medicine cup and said he'd be back shortly.

Asher drank the syrup and, ten minutes later, as predicted,

started to get drunkenly silly. Dr. Liu returned and decisively said, "Okay, let's go, see you in a bit!" scooped him up over his shoulder, and left. Asher was facing us, and I could see his goofy smile for a moment before they disappeared around the corner. Mike and I turned to each other and walked to the waiting room, where we would just quietly sit for the next half hour, watching the clock, not saying a word.

It all turned out okay, just like my little book said it would.

Thank goodness for little books.

In September, when we went back to preschool, he was in a new class with a lot of kids and it was a bit chaotic. After a week, he started telling me at night he didn't want to go, something he'd never done before.

There was another school we'd toured back when we'd first begun the preschool search, a beautiful little Montessori school located in a 1950s schoolhouse. The classrooms were filled with kids quietly doing little "jobs"—their term for activities.* It was actually so quiet that I was slightly spooked? But at recess I could see the children jumping and running and having fun,

---

* I still don't totally understand why they had to call activities "jobs," but if there's one thing I've learned about preschools, it's that every single one of them does at least one thing that makes you wonder, *Why the fuck are they doing that?* and if there are fewer than five of these things it's probably a decent preschool.

and I poked my head into a music class being led by an enthusiastic young man who somehow had a room full of preschoolers playing a song in unison on wooden xylophones. I thought it was the perfect school for my son, but when I read their pamphlet more closely, I saw that they required kids to be potty trained to enroll, and at the time, we were still very much not. So we'd had to pass. Still, I never stopped thinking about this school, even as we attended this other, very nice place filled with very nice people who were willing to change his diapers and help him wipe for two years.

But as the weeks went by, and Asher nervously put his shirt in his mouth every time I dropped him off, I knew the time had come to make the switch. He was potty trained. We could do this. Couldn't we?

I began the little book. Of all the ones I had made so far, his potential reaction to this one terrified me the most. Even if it was no longer the perfect fit, his school had been his second home for as long as he could remember. It was familiar. Familiar was our favorite feeling. As I drew the new school, and me walking him into the classroom, I felt absolute dread, remembering how hard it had been to transition him into school in the first place.

I wrote the phrase I had written so many times before: "Some things will be the same, and some things will be different." I enumerated the things that would be the same—his backpack, being dropped off and picked up and coming home—and touched lightly, but truthfully, on the things that would be different, which was most of it. I drew the little flowers that grew outside the schoolhouse.

I was sure he was going to be upset. What if he said no? And then what? How would I unwind this? Was there a little book about what to do if you made your kid a book about switching schools and he had a nervous breakdown? WHO WAS WRITING LITTLE BOOKS FOR ME???

The afternoon before his last day at the old school, I told Asher I wanted to read him a special little book. We sat on the couch.

I read the words, "Tomorrow will be your last day at your school. After tomorrow you will go to a new school." I held my breath. He looked on, silent. I continued on with the things that would be the same, and the things that would be different (among them, ideally, him not eating his shirt from anxiety every time we walked into the building).

Finally, we got to the end.

He had no questions. "Let's go play Magna-Tiles," he said.

There was nothing like the feeling of Asher's bored quiet at the end of a little book reading. It meant I'd done it. That I had found the safe haiku. That at least some aspect of future life had been turned into a digestible story, a happy story—or at least, one that was happy enough. A beginning, a middle, an ending. Solid ground.

Some things will be the same; some things will be different.

Our first day was in mid-October. Anxious me was so stressed about that first drop-off, but from moment one, Asher loved his new school. He loved doing the little jobs, and he loved the music class. He loved his teachers. Within weeks, I could see how he was blossoming there. He would come home talking about "deciduous forests." He loved that each morning began with his teachers choosing a "person of the day" who would do special tasks, like step outside and offer a weather report to the rest of his friends. In Los Angeles, the report was almost always the same ("it's sunny today"), but he loved doing it. I loved dropping him off there, giving him our special hug, walking out, and then watching him wave proudly through the window— proud that he felt okay to say goodbye. I loved the moment of the wave, and I loved the moment where I would see him actually turn away and go join his friends. To be watching him when he didn't know I was watching was such a thrill—that little glimpse of him when he didn't know I was there, when I felt like I was truly seeing him, growing up out in the world.

The second week of March, the pandemic upended our lives. The school abruptly closed. Asher came home. We thought it would be for a few weeks, maybe a month, but also, we didn't know. The ground beneath our feet felt like it was melting away. Someone emailed us a little printable book for children about the coronavirus, featuring a smiley-faced spike protein holding a suitcase.

"I'm the coronavirus, and I love to travel," I read to Asher in bed, trying to sound calm even though I can actually feel my stomach dropping through the floor. When we were finished reading, Asher was quiet for a moment. Then, for the first time ever, he grabbed the book and angrily threw it across the room.

From March until June, he played with no other children.

By May, it became clear the school year was over. By July, it became clear the next school year wasn't happening either. He would never go back to his beautiful little place.

What can you say? What can you write?

In September, I made a new little book about how we were going to have school in our backyard. I didn't know how to properly draw the Montessori schoolhouse, so I printed out a photo from their website and cried as I taped it to a piece of paper. I drew pictures of the three other children who would be a part of this little learning pod, none of whom he knew. They were the children of work friends of mine, the offspring of families we'd found who agreed on pandemic protocols.

By the time I read him this one, I wasn't worried about how he would react. I knew he was starved for school, for routine, for a teacher.

I think about all of the times in my life I would have loved a little book. A short and simple guide to what was coming, and would stay the same, and what would be different, and how. Or at the very least, some basic guideline of what that ratio might be.

I originally thought the little books were kind of a Zen exercise—an attempt to write confidently, and nonjudgmentally, about what was to come. But now, writing in the middle of a global pandemic, I realize that the whole time I was making little books, I was so focused on boiling everything down to that "safest haiku" that I would sometimes forget that the caveat to every little book is: we have no idea whatsoever about what is going to happen. Just by writing about any version of the future at all, the little books were actually more acts of pure faith, little essays asserting some known reality coming our way.

Somewhere between the optimism of pure faith and the letting go of pure Zen lies, I suppose, good parenting. And probably, while we're at it, just good living. Outside of those two edges lie all of the possible heartbreaks.

But our children need us, at bare minimum, to not be nihilists, right? We have to believe in something. We also have to find some way to tell them things will be okay, no matter what.

How can we want it to be some way and also not need it to be some way?

While I was writing this essay, the one you are reading, Asher, now five, came up to me and said, "I'm worried."

Me: About what?

Him: About what's going to happen.

Me: (panicking) With what?

Him: I don't know, just what's going to happen! No one knows!

I had never seen this in him before, this kind of generalized anxiety about the future. He was becoming more and more like me.

"Well," I said, "that's true. No one knows exactly what's going to happen in the future."

He looked at me, shocked that I didn't have something more comforting to say. I was also shocked. I vamped while I tried to come up with something better.

"Moms and dads do know some things that are gonna happen," I responded.

"LIKE WHAT?" he said.

"Well . . . we know we are always gonna love you and we'll always be a family," I said, and even as I said it, I knew how inadequate it was. He wanted to know that I could reassure him of something else. I racked my brain for something, anything, else, trying to remember lines from my favorite Oprah "What I Know for Sure" columns in her magazine.

Later that night, I lie awake thinking about it. What true little book is there, really?

"We are alive.

"One day we will die.

"Some things will be the same, and some things will be different."

In the dark I think, *What if, when we die, everything is different and nothing is the same?* (That is a terrifying thought.)

Then I think, *What could I write that would make us all feel better?* Maybe:

"Everything will be different, except for the love. The love will be the same."

The Return

There is a stage near the very end of the hero's journey that Campbell calls "the crossing of the return threshold," in which the hero ponders the notion of simply not going back home. Why, having come so far, and worked so hard, would she return to a world that doesn't appreciate her, one that doesn't appreciate what she's learned?

Campbell explains:

"The first problem of the returning hero is to accept as real . . . the passing joys and sorrows, banalities and noisy obscenities of life. Why re-enter such a world? Why attempt to make plausible, or even interesting, to men and women consumed with passion, the experience . . . ? . . . The returning hero, to complete his adventure, must survive the impact of the world."

Motherhood leaves you inevitably and profoundly changed; you can be similar to who you were—maybe?—but you'll never be the same. Some of the changes are easy to embrace: I personally have loved the feeling of being out of fucks to give about so many of the dumb things I gave all my fucks to when I was younger. Others require a more painful adaptation.

At the same time, you're also aware that upon attempting to reenter normal life from mom-land or middle-aged-land, or both, you'll be seen as a weirdo, or cranky, or stubborn, or all of the above. Doesn't it make sense you'd think about just not going back?

The end of the hero's journey is like the path of a rocket reentering Earth's atmosphere. It must burn. Pieces blister and break off. You're not the same, splashing down into the ocean, as when you left. When you took off, your boosters were ablaze, fueling the epic push of new life out of yourself and into Earth's orbit. Everyone at mission control stood and applauded.

But the return is more like free fall. The rocket that lands in the ocean doesn't look like the one that departed. It's a little pod-like thing, a charred husk of what took off. Instead of wings spreading, a parachute awkwardly collapses into the water, a butterfly in reverse. What's left is this metal shell, just a nub of what was there before. And yet—it's a nub that's been to space, for fuck's sake.

Just surviving is the success.

So much of who I was—my daily habits, my identifying clothing—had to get thrown away in making room to become a mother. What's left of me is now sharing space with a little boy, and as a result, my mental capacity has been reduced from a decent three bed/two bath apartment to, at best, a little tenement studio. While the tight space creates some cons, the pro is that what can come in, and what cannot, is pretty clear.

Some Things I Don't Have Room For:

Harry Styles: I cannot make room in my brain for Harry Styles. For the first few years of the growing Styles storm, I thought, *The guy from One Direction? Surely this cannot be right.* Then he started dressing like everyone's mother's wildest friend from the '70s, and people seemed to get even more excited. The world has been demanding that I need to know about Harry Styles and pay attention to Harry Styles, but nevertheless, #I'veresisted. At the moment I'm writing these words, the universe is freshly abuzz over his performance at the 2021 Grammys, where he sang his song "Watermelon Sugar," which—I SEE YOU, Harry Styles—is about eating pussy, I getttt itrrrrr. He wore leather bell bottoms and a leather blazer top with no shirt which looked admittedly quite nice. However, he was also sporting a green boa around his neck, which was a bridge too far for me. He did remove it halfway through the performance, but by then the impression was made. And I can't help but imagine there was a discussion AROUND the boa before, like, clearly he wanted the big moment where he tossed the boa to the ground and most likely a team of stylists sourced multiple boas to present as options. For me, this is all a big turnoff.

I feel similarly about his rings. For as long as I can remember. I've had a thing about men who wear lots of rings. It's not that I'm judging, and I do think it can look cool, but I can't help but picture the moment of them putting them on in the morning one by one or taking them off one by one at night, and I want to hide under the bed, I'm so embarrassed.

The deep down of it, though, is that really all I can think about when I look at Harry Styles is how much I would have loved him when I was twenty-one and how deeply I am certain he would have hurt my FEELINGS. From my middle-aged perch all I can think is: Sorry, but I am not falling for it, Harry Styles. I am not gonna be Charlie Brown trying to kick that football because I know Lucy pulls it away every time. I mean if you get a chance to ride the Styles carousel I'm sure it's a GREAT time, but still. I know a celebrity crush is supposed to just be a fantasy, but truthfully I simply can't handle this dude rejecting even my pretend secret feelings.

I just can't have a crush on anyone under thirty now, and if I'm being honest I think forty-eight is my floor. At the moment my most consistent celebrity romantic interest is Andy Slavitt, the former chief COVID advisor to President Biden who many of us got to know as a calm voice of reason on Twitter during an unrelenting shit storm. Every time he tweets out the number of Americans who have been vaccinated, I wonder, Does he have a wife?*

Billie Eilish: Let me start by saying that I know when I was fourteen I would have BEEN OBSESSED with Billie Eilish. Or at least, I think I would have, I can't be sure because I have

---

* JUST GOOGLED AND OF COURSE HE DOES.

listened to not one note of her music. I am aware that this is probably MY LOSS. And yet—I simply do not have room for Billie Eilish in my ruin of a brain. She is everywhere I look: on the cover of *Vanity Fair*, on my many little favorite webbysites, and on the same Grammys where Harry Styles is singing about watermelon pussy. When I look at her green hair and long nails and I wanna say webbed clothing?, I feel as if we are on different planets. To be clear, I am well aware that the planet she is from is very much Earth and the planet I am from is now the one that's light-years away and can only be seen in perfect night weather conditions with no light pollution. The point is, I just cannot let Billie Eilish in anymore. I am now in the throes of middle-aged angst, not teenage angst, and nothing makes my current angst spike higher than the notion of feeling nostalgia for my younger self's angst.

TikTok: I was already about twenty social media apps behind when TikTok emerged. Somewhere around Snapchat, I decided I just couldn't keep up. I never felt bad about my decision to stop downloading each and every new messaging app, each new public-facing modality. None of them sounded that interesting to me, or at best, they all seemed kinda similar to the ones I already had? I mean, how many different apps does one need to tell one's partner, DONT FORGET 2 PICK UP KIDS' RASH CREAM?*

Then TikTok came along and, as with Styles and Eilish, people seemed CRANKED UP about it. I'm not so wretchedly old

---

* The answer is one.

that I'm not curious when I hear a kerfuffle, so I figured maybe I would take a quick peekaroo at this one app. And lo and behold, people do seem to be having a great time in there. I mean, there's a lot of booty short dancing, and that is indeed quite fun. And yet I don't fully understand it, and I will never be on there. It feels a bit like a party I'm not invited to, even though technically we're all invited; it's probably more accurate to say it feels like a party I shouldn't have been invited to. I can only look at like three of these videos before I stagger backward, just gobsmacked; how are all of these people PERFORMING their lives with this level of ENERGY all the time? I think at age forty-five-almost-six, I just feel a bit performed out, maybe because so much of my non-TikTok life in the last several years—specifically being a mother and having to pretend I know what I'm doing—has felt like one long, relentlessly unending show, that I'm just quite excited to not do a show whenever possible.

Which brings me to the deep gratitude I feel for where I am currently at in my journey: Once you are as physically, emotionally, and spiritually drained as the average mother, eliminating the obligations and performances of your youth is so much easier; nay, their elimination is essential. There are so many things I just can't get it up to do anymore, and even if I could, wouldn't.

Some Things I Don't Miss:

Waiting on line for brunch: Why did I ever wait on line for brunch? What a wildly stupid thing that now seems to do.

The one meal I actually know how to make is breakfast. Why did I ever need to wait in line for someone to make it for me? Welp . . . okay. I guess the answer is that I wanted to look at attractive cool people eating brunch while I ate my brunch. But now I feel like I've seen all the attractive cool people I need to see for the rest of my life; or at least, I no longer feel the need to try to see them in person. I'm fine to look at attractive cool people on my phone while I eat my son's leftover pancakes standing over the sink. Please don't get me wrong—I'm not trying to pretend I don't still enjoy brunch out with a friend. I do. It's just that now, on the rare occasion I am able to bail on my child in the middle of the day, we need to get our butts in seats and drinks in hands IMMEDIATELY, because the clock is ticking on how long someone's watching the kid and our lives aren't gonna grouse about themselves.

Wishing I was the prettiest in the room: All through my early twenties, whenever I walked into a party or a meeting or any kind of social gathering, I would always have a "moment before" where I secretly hoped I would be among the prettier people in it. I guess I was hoping I'd be viewed as a nine if enough fives were present, which was very much the hope of someone who viewed herself as a six at best. I'm very embarrassed to be admitting this, but it's true, and insofar as we live in a society that couldn't make it clearer that pretty/thin is the primary expectation of young women, I don't blame myself. And even though intellectually I knew better, on a gut level, I couldn't ignore that society wanted me to measure myself against other women, and to calculate my value through the lens of whatever man stags might be, quite literally, dicking around. I would walk into a room of pretty girls and ache with jealousy, crushed by the pain of never winning the Pretty Contest, even though it is unwinnable by design. There is something so comforting now about being completely out of that race—which is not to say I don't think I'm still pretty in my own forty-six-year-old cake-loving way, but just that I feel so firmly out of the contest, that now when I see some kind of weapons-grade Zoë Kravitz young beauty, my mind actually just lies back and enjoys it like I would a vacation sunset. Like how LUCKY am I that I exist at a time when Zoë Kravitz's face exists, wowowowowow.

Apologizing all the time: If I had to name my NUMBER ONE thing that I do not miss in my newfound Middle Age, it is, hands all the way fucking down, reflexively apologizing to people who have made me feel bad, in order to protect them from feeling bad. It took almost forty years, but I have slowly unlearned this instinctive *I'm sorry*-ing that once fell from my mouth umpteen times a day—the *oh, sorry* you say to a man who bumps you on line for coffee because you were in the way; the *sorry, this is probably dumb* as a way of laying the groundwork for your ideas to be dismissed immediately after you say them at work. I FIVE STARS Highly Recommend to all women at any stage of life just going cold turkey on self-loathing *I'm sorry*s, but I will also say, if you happen to have a child around, being a mom can be great practice for no longer suffering others' bullshit. There are so many moments where you have to voice your kid's needs to exactly the kind of adult who would have steamrolled you in the past. I've found it much easier to say *go* *fuck right off* when dealing with someone who is diminishing my child, or *fucking excuse me, but I need you to pay attention* to someone who is supposed to be helping my kid but isn't. My ability to stop being polite and start getting real *The Real World*™ is so much stronger when I use it on Asher's behalf than I ever found it when trying to use it on behalf of myself.

All of this is to simply suggest: that from the deeply protective ferocity with which we stand up for our children, we could learn a lot about standing up for ourselves. It's one of the innumerable unexpected insights that comes from being on this whole trip, a chance power we can pick up as we continue stumbling forward, toward ... what, exactly? Why are we doing this? What are we supposed to be getting OUT of this journey?

Almost every classic hero myth ends with the protagonist returning from her adventure with, as Campbell puts it, "the ultimate boon." What is the ultimate boon of motherhood? What is a boon at all? It's an etymologically odd little word, derived from a Norse word for "prayer," although it later came to mean "a gift or favor." It went from meaning the thing that was asked for, to the thing that was given. There's a sticky little tension there, because of course what you ask for and what you receive are not always exactly the same thing.

I remember one dark night in Las Vegas, years ago. Not what you'd think—I was there for work. Truth be told, I'm basically allergic to Vegas. This particular visit came a few days after my doctor had just informed me that I might never be able to have a baby. Per her instructions, I'd immediately gone off of birth control, and my body was in shock. I was sweaty and nauseous and would experience waves of hot pins and needles tingling through my limbs. Unable to sleep, I watched local TV news at three thirty in the morning as party lights shimmered off the walls, making the room feel like a fish tank. I remember praying as hard as I had ever prayed for anything that somehow, I would be able to have a child. Nowhere in my prayer was I thinking about what having a child would entail. The bone-deep fatigue. The mental exhaustion. The endless fury. The ridiculous fighting. The so much crying and so much begging in the so many bathrooms. The harrowing tantrums he had when he was three, where he would attack me with his fists until I pinned him to the floor. The isolation. The frustration at my body for refusing to look the way it once had. The complete transformation of every single atom from this Known Me Before into this Unknown Me After.

Believe it or not, I did not specify any of that in my prayer.

And yet. When I think about the hero being graced with this boon . . .

I mean, of course . . . the boon is my son.

But also . . . maybe this metamorphosis has been the boon.

There is something I feel when my boy holds my hand. It is simultaneously the most blissed out I feel as a mother, and the most terrified I feel as the regular human person that, somewhere inside, I still am. His trust, his full belief that I am the person to lead him somehow always creates an electric thrill;

in his little grip I feel my old self and my new self spark, as if two wires touched. There is the old self who isn't sure I should be leading anyone, or anything, anywhere. We hold hands as we cross the street, or go up the stairs, or lie in bed at night, and the question lingers. Can I believe in myself the way he believes in me?

The old self isn't sure.

And then there is the new self that knows, with profound certainty: yes. Yes, because, I can do this. I did it yesterday, and the day before that, and I did it today, and I know I will do it tomorrow. I've been pushed past every edge I thought was my limit, and still, I stayed. To stay I had to go down deep, deep, deeper than I knew existed within me. Into the belly of the whale; down to the bottom of the ocean; back to the supermarket for Nom-Noms for the ten thousandth time.

I have a vision of us meeting for lunch decades from now, when I'm sixty-eight and he's twenty-seven. We meet at Cafe Cluny in New York, near where I grew up. It's a rainy fall day outside, but here between us it's as warm as can be. I have gray hair and big glasses, he's handsome in a sweater. We laugh as he tells me funny stories about his friends, his job, this new person he loves.

The ultimate boon.

I believe.

Acknowledgments

This has been quite a time to be writing a book, or doing anything really, and I could not have done it without the help of so many lovely people.

Thank you to my editor, Emily Griffin, who bought me a glass of red wine a million years ago and asked if I might be interested in writing something one day. I am so grateful for your endless kindness and brilliance. Thank you to Jonathan Burnham and to the entire team at HarperCollins for doulaing this project into existence.

Eternal thanks to the world's best, most dashing book agent, David Kuhn, for believing in me all these years. Nate Muscato, thank you for your steady support and endless good cheer on the subway.

Giant thank-you and eternal hug to my manager, friend, and all-around stunning human Christie Smith for your wisdom and the most necessary constant contact.

Thank you, Tim Phillips and Brian Lazarus, for gracefully

dealing with all the stuff my brain isn't capable of dealing with, which is most stuff.

Kate Grodd. There aren't enough words to fully express what you mean to me so I'll just say: I could not do this life without you. You are, quite simply, an ICON.

Undying love forever to Zubeida Ullah, Maura Madden, and Becky Kutys. Thank you for your decades of friendship and humor, for your beautiful, amazing souls, and 24–7 text support.

Special thank you to Casey Wilson: you invited me into a baby music group in your home six years ago and ever since you have been an absolute MASTER CLASS on writing, creating, and joie de vivre-ing while mothering. I am so thankful to know you.

Oh hello, Liz Feldman. Thank you for taking the time to read early stages of these words; you made them way better. I'm so grateful for your friendship and your brilliant mind.

And to the coven of Celeste Hughey, Kelly Hutchinson, Madie Dhaliwal, and Cara DiPaolo: oh, how I love you gorgeous witches.

Emily Ryan Lerner and Jenn Hwang, thank you for being in the foxhole with me.

A big emotional thank-you to my dear friends Becky Sloviter and Eric Blume for being such giant warm hearts and enthusiastic cheerleaders.

To Lara Hillier: thank you for your endless support, thoughtful presence, and for helping me with this book; you helped me over the finish line right when I thought I couldn't go another step. You are just a gosh darn gift of a gal.

Acknowledgments

Thank you to the entire staff of the Bowery Hotel for making such a beautiful, comfy place exist and for giving this bedraggled mom a room upgrade at a really clutch moment.

I am forever indebted to Lucy Sibrian for taking care of my boy with such tenderness and grace. You make our whole family better. We love you.

To Asher's first nanny, Luz Antonelli: when we moved away, Asher was six months old, and I heard you whisper to him when we said goodbye, "You won't remember me, but I'll never forget you." We will never forget you either. We still read about Monty and the Forget-Me-Nots and think of you every time.

To the night nurses who took care of us after Asher was born—I am grateful to each of you to this day.

I feel it's important to say: This book was written largely during 2020, when the COVID-19 pandemic began. Thank you to all the nurses, doctors, scientists, and essential workers around the globe who have worked tirelessly to lift us through this. A very special thank-you to New York City's best doctor, Jahangir Rahman, who offered to do a house call when my mother got sick in March 2020. I still tear up thinking about it. And a very special thank-you to New York City's best OB-GYN, Tani Sanghvi, who took care of me not just as a patient, but as a whole person, for so many years, and delivered my son into this world.

To Mike: I love you. Thank you for being the greatest father and most steady partner on the planet.

Michal, David, and Beth: I am so lucky you're my family. Thank you for always being there. I love you tons.

Mom and Da: I always thought I knew how incredibly hard you worked to take care of us . . . but until I became a mom, I didn't *really* know. I probably still don't totally know? But I know more. You were both in my heart the entire journey of this book. I love you. You are my heroes.

And to Asher, my beautiful, sweet boy.

As I tell you every night: I'm so proud to be your mama. And I'm so proud you're my son.

I love you beyond measure.

About the Author

Jessi Klein is the author of *You'll Grow Out of It* and the Emmy and Peabody award–winning head writer and an executive producer of Comedy Central's critically acclaimed series *Inside Amy Schumer*. She is an actor and consulting producer on the hit Netflix show *Big Mouth*, and has also written for Netflix's *Dead to Me* and Amazon's *Transparent* as well as *Saturday Night Live*. Klein has been featured on the popular storytelling series *The Moth*, and has been a regular panelist on NPR's *Wait Wait... Don't Tell Me!* Her work has been published in the *New York Times*, the *New Yorker*, *GQ*, and *Cosmopolitan*, and she has her own half-hour Comedy Central stand-up special. She lives in Los Angeles with her family.